The Ivory Tower

The Ivory Tower

Perspectives of Women of Color in Higher Education

Edited by Kimetta R. Hairston
and Tawannah G. Allen

ROWMAN & LITTLEFIELD
Lanham • Boulder • New York • London

Published by Rowman & Littlefield
An imprint of The Rowman & Littlefield Publishing Group, Inc.
4501 Forbes Boulevard, Suite 200, Lanham, Maryland 20706
www.rowman.com

86-90 Paul Street, London EC2A 4NE

British Library Cataloguing in Publication Information Available

Library of Congress Cataloging-in-Publication Data
Names: Hairston, Kimetta, 1970- editor. | Allen, Tawannah G., editor.
Title: The ivory tower : perspectives of women of color in higher education
  / edited by Kimetta R. Hairston and Tawannah G. Allen.
Description: Lanham, Maryland: Rowman & Littlefield, [2023] | Includes
  bibliographical references and index. | Summary: "Women of color in the
  academe often face the double-jeopardy of race and gender bias. The
  Ivory Tower features firsthand accounts of BIPOC women in academia in
  order to promote the recruitment, retention, and success of women of
  color in higher education institutions. Topics include socio-emotional
  preservation, mentorship, and authentic identity"— Provided by publisher.
Subjects: LCSH: African American women—Education (Higher)—Case
  studies. | African American women—Education (Graduate)—Case studies.
  | African American women college administrators—Case studies. | African
  American women college teachers—Case studies. | Discrimination in
  higher education. | Sex discrimination in higher education. | Feminism and
  education.
Classification: LCC LC2781 .I86 2023 (print) | LCC LC2781 (ebook) |
  DDC 378.0082—dc23/eng/20220805
LC record available at https://lccn.loc.gov/2022029056
LC ebook record available at https://lccn.loc.gov/2022029057

ISBN: 978-1-4758-6823-4 (cloth)
ISBN: 978-1-4758-6824-1 (pbk.)
ISBN: 978-1-4758-6825-8 (ebook)

Contents

Foreword, *Linda C. Tillman*   ix

Acknowledgments   xiii

Introduction: Empowering Women of Color in Academia   1
    Kimetta R. Hairston and Tawannah G. Allen

PART I   BEGINNING THE JOURNEY IN ACADEMIA

1 Watching and Waiting to Exhale: Affirming Black Women
    in Academia   7
    Ayanna M. Lynch, Kim Brittingham Barnett,
    and Makeba T. Green

2 From Underdog to Accomplished: Persevering through
    Unexpected Challenges   25
    Nina Jacks

3 Resilience: A Prideful Term of Perseverance and
    Descriptor of Unspoken Challenges Endured   39
    Bianca Nixon, Diamond Melendez, and Comfort Boateng

4 "Voluntold": A Framework for Contextualizing
    Black Women's Negative Experiences in the Academy   55
    Marie Parfait-Davis

PART II   ADVANCING THROUGH

5   The Work We Must Do: Toward an Understanding of
    How Early Career Black Women Faculty Navigate
    Their Place in Higher Education   71
    Miyoshi Juergensen and Tamela C. Thomas

6   Lost and Found: A Tale of Two Black Women
    Seeking Solidarity within Academia   81
    Erica-Brittany Horhn and Sharon Lassiter

7   From Clinical to Tenure-Track Faculty:
    Scholarly Reflections of Teaching and Learning   93
    Joy L. Kennedy

PART III   MENTORSHIP OR SPONSORSHIP

8   Engineer or Test Pilot: Naming and Claiming a Successful
    Mentoring Relationship   103
    Yolanda F. Holt

9   The Importance of Developing Effective Mentor-Mentee
    Relationships in Academia: The Perspectives of Two
    Women of Color in STEM   113
    Angela D. Broadnax and Verónica A. Segarra

10 Bringing in Afrocentric Values to Mentor
    African American Students   125
    Annie Ruth Leslie

11 Latina Identity and Belonging in Academia   141
    Mariela A. Rodríguez

PART IV   THRIVING . . . NOT JUST SURVIVING

12 I Ain't Sorry: Establishing Boundaries in the Pursuit of
    Wholeness with JOY   151
    Brandi Hinnant-Crawford

13 No Crystal Stair: Black Women Reaching Landings
and Turning Corners in Library and Information Science   159
Shamella Cromartie and Shaundra Walker

14 Triple Threat: Thriving as a Black Woman Mathematician   171
Dandrielle Lewis

15 Getting Published: A Black Woman's Journey to Tenure
and Promotion   185
Dionne V. McLaughlin

Afterword, *Aminta H. Breaux*   195

Index   201

About the Editors and Contributors   213

Foreword

The Ivory Tower: Perspectives of Women of Color in Higher Education is the right book for a time such as this. It is the right book to nourish the souls of women of color in higher education. It is the right book at a time when women, especially women of color, in higher education are navigating the triple pandemics of racism, sexism, and COVID-19. As women of color continue to survive and thrive in their ivory towers, this is the right book for a time such as this.

Chapters in this book touch on several important themes. These themes are common to discussions about women in general but are especially applicable to women of color in higher education. Perseverance, resilience, and determination. Race, class, gender, and intersectionality. Sisterhood, support systems, and mentoring. And of course, career advancement—promotion and tenure, promotion to full professor, and advancement to administrative careers. These authors write about these and other themes to send a clear message: while life in the ivory tower is not always a crystal stair, we still rise. Indeed, this is the right book for such a time as this.

Contributors in this book describe some of the persistent challenges faced by women—particularly women of color—in higher education. These challenges have gained a great deal of attention in the aftermath of the Nikole Hannah-Jones story, and much has been written in publications including journal articles, higher-education newsletters, and opinion pieces. For example, Rucks-Ahidiana (2021) wrote an opinion piece in *Inside Higher Ed* about the obstacles faced by Black women as they work toward promotion and tenure.

Several contributors in this book also write about the numerous obstacles Black women face, and like Rucks-Ahidiana, they point to issues of gender, race, and age discrimination as well as inequitable and uneven promotion and tenure policies that place Black women and other women of color in situations that their White colleagues would rarely, if ever, experience. Constant macroaggressions, devaluing of their scholarship, being overloaded with committee assignments, and being forced to be the "race expert" are just a few of the challenges faced by BIPOC women in higher education.

In a September 2021 article titled "Universities Say They Want More Diverse Faculties: So Why Is Academia Still So White?" Matias and colleagues mention several key points about people of color in the academy: the academy has a problem with race; Black, Latinx, American Indian, and multiracial faculty are underrepresented in the tenured faculty ranks; there has been little progress on faculty diversity initiatives for tenured and tenure-track faculty; the rule-makers make rules that work well for Whites but not for faculty of color; and even when funds are made available to support retention, this often does not work because faculty of color face hostile work environments where their intellectual contributions and their humanity are undervalued. These challenges are very similar to some of the challenges discussed by contributors in this book.

Several of the contributors expertly use critical frameworks and methodologies to interrogate policies, practices, and procedures in higher education and their impact on BIPOC women. The use of feminist theories and frameworks, critical autoethnography, and intersectional frameworks add to the sense of urgency to tell their stories and to speak their truths.

As noted by several contributors in this book, women of color are *expected* to assume numerous roles. They are *expected* to mentor other minority colleagues as well as diverse or minority students. They are *expected* to be superwoman, other-mothers, and DEI experts all while, as one author notes, they are often "seatless in the situation rooms." And in many cases, while being overburdened with these expectations, women—particularly women of color—have little time to conduct research and write for publication, two of the most important requirements for career advancement in higher education. Thus, working toward career advancement often becomes a secondary rather than a primary focus of the job for women of color.

The importance of mentoring in higher education cannot be over-stated, and this is also a prominent theme in this book. Research suggests that minority women in higher education are often excluded from formal and informal mentoring relationships (Tillman, 2018). They often lack access to networks and to mentors who can give them advice and guidance about research, teaching, writing for publication, and grant writing; recommend them for important committee assignments; and give them strategies that will lead to a successful path to promotion and tenure, promotion to full professor, and administrative advancement.

Authors also discuss the challenges of cross-race and cross-gender mentoring. However, since BIPOC women and people of color generally are severely underrepresented at all levels of higher education, cross-race and cross-gender mentoring must be a consideration in any mentoring plan. Additionally, mentoring relationships for minority women must be reconceptualized as a relationship of equals rather than a superior-subordinate relationship. As contributors in this book emphasize, mentoring can play a vital role in the career success of BIPOC women in higher education.

Minority female graduate students also have a story to tell. Their experiences as students who also must navigate the often-unwelcome and hostile spaces of higher education are illustrative of how the challenges faced by BIPOC women in higher education start at the under-graduate level and usually continue throughout graduate school. Their experiences as minority students on White campuses, their interactions with White professors, and their emphasis on forming meaningful mentoring relationships give us insight into the struggles and successes of these students. Like BIPOC women faculty and administrators, they too exhibit resilience, perseverance, and determination.

And finally, contributors in this book tell us that women of color in higher education want to do more than just survive in these spaces that are often not made for them—spaces where they are marginalized, silenced, and expected to "stay in their place." But as noted in the last chapter of this book, women of color boldly proclaim that they *are* in their place, they *are* in the spaces where they belong, and they *will* "protect and preserve their health, peace and joy while being in the academy." And while our journeys as women of color in higher education are different and not always a crystal stair, we still rise. This is the right book for such a time as this.

Linda C. Tillman, PhD
Professor Emerita, University of North Carolina–Chapel Hill

REFERENCES

Matias, J. Nathan, Neil Lewis Jr., and Elan Hope. 2021, September 7. "Universities Say They Want More Diverse Faculties. So Why Is Academia Still So White?" *FiveThirtyEight*. https://fivethirtyeight.com/features/universities -say-they-want-more-diverse-faculties-so-why-is-academia-still-so-white.

Rucks-Ahidiana, Z. 2021, July 16. "The Systemic Scarcity of Tenured Black Women." *Inside Higher Ed.* www.insidehighered.com/advice/2021/07/16/ black-women-face-many-obstacles-their-efforts-win-tenure-opinion.

Tillman, L. C. 2018. "Achieving Racial Equity in Higher Education: The Case for Mentoring Faculty of Color." *Teachers College Record Yearbook* 120, no. 14: 1–18.

Acknowledgments

The Ivory Tower: Perspectives of Women of Color in Higher Education tells the stories of how women of color impact academia and higher education. We are grateful for the dedication and spirit of this collaboration of the women of color in this book, who have laid their hearts on the line and inspired everyone with their experiences and voices. They share their research, expertise, and compassion as they illuminate the personal and professional experiences of women of color in academia. This book is truly a "team of teams," and we appreciate all of your time and your talents that you have shared in the creation of this book.

To help craft the book, we decided as an editorial team to allow flexibility in the style and writing of each chapter in order to preserve each author's voice. We could not have produced this book without relying on the great works of scholarly authors in a wide variety of fields. Moreover, numerous female colleagues from various universities across the nation offered valuable time to peer review and edit the chapters. We thank all of the peer reviewers and editors. Your feedback was instrumental in making this book a stellar piece of work.

It is a wonderful time to be a woman of color, as we are witnessing history in real time as more women of color are taking on roles in the world that would have never been imagined in the past. We would be remiss if we did not mention that as we prepare this book for publication, Judge Ketanji Brown Jackson—the African American daughter of public school teachers—has broken another barrier, by being confirmed as the next associate justice of the Supreme Court of the United States. While the authors spotlight systemic racial, educational, and societal disparities and challenges among women of color, Judge Brown Jackson is the epitome of how women—particularly Black women—can still rise to the highest positions, despite disparate treatment by those who feel challenged when strength, confidence, and intelligence are exhibited by anyone other than a White male. We hope that this book will enable its readers to "do better when you know better," to ask the tough questions and demand change that will edify and amplify women of color from all ages, across cultural and education levels. A true paradigm shift is needed to understand the power women of color wield in the workplace.

As an editorial team, we want to give special thanks to our project manager assistant, Ms. Tiffany Eller. She helped to keep us and the book's contributors organized and motivated. We could not have done this without her! We are excited about her future as a young scholar. Look out, world! She has arrived!

We would like to give a special acknowledgment to award-winning educator and leader Dr. Linda C. Tillman, who took time to write the foreword from the lens as an expert and woman of color who has experiences similar to those of the contributing authors and beyond. We would also like to acknowledge Dr. Aminta H. Breaux, president of Bowie State University (a Historically Black College/University). She wrote the afterword and provided insight as the first Black woman president in 152 years, as she shared her experiences and challenges as she rose through the ranks in academia.

Finally, no endeavor is complete without thanking God, who guided us through this process and led us to the final book. We would like to dedicate this book to our families and friends who supported us throughout this process. Thank you for your love!

Introduction
Empowering Women of Color in Academia
Kimetta R. Hairston and Tawannah G. Allen

It has become a fashionable trend to talk about supporting women of color who are faculty members and administrators in higher education. How do we hire them? How do we retain them? While colleges and universities often look first to improving recruitment efforts, some of the biggest obstacles for retaining women of color occur in an area that is often overlooked: the university's culture and climate. As a result, retention efforts can be nullified when the obstacles—often not caused by women faculty of color—are allowed to run rampant.

Women of color are underrepresented in college faculty and staff, which contributes to a lack of diversity, equity, and inclusion in teaching practices and curriculum, as well as a lack of role models and support systems for students. According to Vasquez Heilig and colleagues (2019), in 2017, 5.2 percent of tenured faculty at bachelor-degree-granting schools were Black and just 6.6 percent were Latinx. The experiences of women of color in academia are missing from the literature. With this understanding, this book's four parts will encompass the narratives of BIPOC women and their varied experiences within higher education.

Given many people's myopic view of obstacles for diverse faculty, a lot of people tune out at the mere mention of culture and climate, assuming it has no relevance to success at all. That is a grave mistake, as the voices of women of color themselves are saying/yelling/screaming that the university's culture is getting in the way of their retention and their ascension to the rank of full professor. When institutions ignore those voices by continuing to overlook the obstacles and experiences of women of color in higher education, they continue to systematically derail their success. Hearing and understanding the first-hand accounts of women of color is a critical component in the recruitment, retention, and success of women of color. This book serves as a platform for allowing women of color to share their narratives and is divided into four parts:

- Part I: Beginning the Journey in Academia: Contributors discuss topics around promotion and tenure challenges, being the "only one in the room," and advancing to leadership positions. They will also discuss the application and interview processes when applying for practitioner and higher-education positions.
- Part II: Advancing Through: Contributors, including graduate students, discuss their experiences with other students, faculty, and programmatic practices that impact women of color. Topics around gender equality, racism, and sexism will be explored. Contributors discuss the challenges and successes in collaborative research, publications, and grant opportunities.
- Part III: Mentorship or Sponsorship: Contributors discuss mentoring experiences in higher education, through either the lens of a doctoral student or that of a mentor or mentee. This section shares research on the effectiveness of having female/male mentors (from another culture or race). They will talk about the benefits of having a mentor, or when the mentor and mentee do not connect.
- Part IV: Thriving . . . Not Just Surviving: Contributors discuss when BIPOC women are identified by others as the experts and authority on all things culture, race, gender, diversity, and inclusion. They discuss strategies around how to navigate the system of being a woman of color in higher education and in the professional world, advancing to administrative roles, and specific examples of successful advancement in their careers. Once success is granted (e.g., making tenure, advancing to leadership roles, etc.), how do they reach back and make sure that they guide aspiring and novice educators through the process?

While it is important to acknowledge that women of color in the academe often face the double jeopardy of race and gender bias, our contributors' personal experiences tout critical themes paramount for responding to these biases. As they rightfully take their place in higher education, the themes—establishing boundaries to promote socioemotional preservation, recognizing the value of mentorship, becoming resilient during the journey, and acknowledging one's identity to be one's authentic self—are tightly woven throughout the chapters.

It should be noted that the contributors to this book are diverse in age, rank, leadership experiences, length of service in higher education, as well as the type of their institution (e.g., predominantly White or historically Black, public or private). Yet the aforementioned themes are consistent across their narratives. This affirms that despite these differences, the experiences of minority women in higher education are often indistinguishable.

As you journey through the experiences and the perspectives of the contributors, it is our hope that you will not only become enlightened by their stories but also connect with them—both personally and professionally—on many levels in higher education and beyond.

REFERENCE

Vasquez Heilig, Julian, Isabell Wong Flores, Alicia Eileen Barros Souza, Joseph Carlton Barry, and Selene Barceló Monroy. 2019. "Considering the Ethnoracial and Gender Diversity of Faculty in United States College and University Intellectual Communities." *Hispanic Journal of Law & Policy*: 1–31. http://stcl.edu/Journals/HispanicLaw/2019/2019Heilig1-31.pdf.

Part I

BEGINNING THE JOURNEY IN ACADEMIA

Watching and Waiting to Exhale
Affirming Black Women in Academia
Ayanna M. Lynch, Kim Brittingham Barnett, and Makeba T. Green

WHEN WE SEE US

Most Black women typically identify themselves as *Black women*, not *women who are Black*. This is significant because it reflects how their layered identities are prioritized as well as how the world receives them. Black women honor Black lives, stand by leaders of the Black community, along with Black fathers, husbands, brothers, and sons. Inherently, they understand that focusing on their "womanness," or "women's issues," as they apply to Black women, would dilute the Black movement, as it would call attention to themselves and not the communities they have, historically, been culturally and institutionalized to support.

In summary, Black women attempting to support themselves detracts from the overall Black movement. When supporting women's rights issues, Black women may find themselves standing alone, as they sorely lack any reciprocal support systems for themselves. They face the daily dichotomy of some Black men not readily rallying around social justice concerns; likewise, there are no influential masses of White women running to defend Black women. It is this juxtaposition that splinters Black women and diminishes their personhood, and their womanhood, leaving little to no choice when doing whatever is possible to preserve one's full humanity.

Given this margin of choice, Black women may either further the agenda of Black men or White women while their own gets crumpled and kicked to the wayside. It is within this historical and cultural context that the stage is set for the uphill battle many Black women faculty continue to fight in academia. This struggle is both internal, by battling self-doubt and disbelief, and external, by bearing the grit of cultivating the pearl that is the fine art of diplomacy toward their colleagues. Often this occurs through lessons of disaster averted, deceit, and despair—all in the name of finding what, at times, seems an impossible path toward a seat at the table of progress.

Black feminist thought (Hill Collins 2000; hooks 1989; Lorde 2020) addresses this cognitive dissonance as the complex relationships between the individual and society, or between human agency and social structures. Issues of power and stratification are significant to studies of intersectionality (Crenshaw 2017). Black feminist thought is grounded in intersectionality central to resistance, activism, and politics of empowerment (Alinia 2015).

According to Hill Collins (2000), there are five distinguishing features of Black feminist thought. This chapter highlights two of these features: (1) intersectionality of gender, race, and age central to mentorship, sponsorship, and evaluation, and (2) collective identity produced out of the tension of oppression and resistance. Black women have a history of storytelling. "It is part of how we position and reposition ourselves in spaces that routinely try to convince us that we are disposable; how we resist and redefine; a vehicle whereby we explore and develop epistemologies built upon centuries of lived experience" (Sinclair-Chapman 2019).

Black women are apprehensive about telling their truths because history has shown them that their stories are lost on others—they are neither heard nor valued nor supported. Often, Black women's narratives do not resonate with others, and they do not interest them, especially when their experiences do not support others' agendas. Additionally, sharing themselves has been costly. Doing so comes from a place of vulnerability—which, all too often, has been exploited. The tragedy and triumph of Nikole Hannah-Jones is the most notable example of this struggle (Carter and Craig 2022).

Black women ultimately move from openness to regret, due to disappointment about what has—or has not—been done, including missed or blocked opportunities. Instead of confessions, Black women make concessions that protect others and not themselves. But the authors contend that Black women's silence won't protect them. It only invites further harm by emboldening the oppressor.

In other instances, Black women are reluctant to testify because they are "protectors." They willingly, lovingly, and proudly protect everything sacred to them—their families and communities—often at the cost of their self-preservation. Professionally, they protect at the expense of everything they sacrificed to earn their rightful place at the tenure and promotion table. They perennially have the backs of their colleagues, departments, and institutions, yet they grin and bear the pain of being overlooked, underpaid, and overworked.

For example, many Black women faculty are *voluntold* to do much of the grunt work, particularly the service and leadership that no one else wants to do or, when asked, many respectfully decline. However, such contributions are practically negligible during tenure and promotion deliberations, and furthermore, these women are often targets of sharp critique by colleagues and the administration. This is part of the "Superwoman Complex": doing everything and enduring everything. *Cue Chaka and Whitney as Black women collectively adjust their capes.*

How and why do Black women seeking tenure or promotion at HBCUs find themselves as "outsiders"? Sinclair-Chapman (2019) maintains that the tenure process intrinsically creates these power dynamics; it relies heavily on "the subjective evaluations of insiders of a relatively powerless outsider" and serves as the gateway drug for academic bullying and other violent behaviors in the academy. These boundaries and behaviors are not only destructive but also especially threatening to Black women in the academy. The plethora of research in this area describes the experience and often-grim fate of Black women on this journey for validation through tenure and promotion in academic rank at PWIs (Daut 2019; Hinton 2010; Porter et al. 2020; Lee and Leonard 2001). However, the collective experiences and research of Black female faculty has revealed that equally disheartening experiences occur at HBCUs (del Priore 2022).

HBCUs are often regarded as places of refuge, comfort, and support for students and educators of color to shine. HBCUs are known for excellence, innovation, conversation, teaching, affirmation, and forging authentic relationships between faculty members. Yet, for many Black female faculty, the pursuit of professional advancement can ultimately dim their light, mute their voices, and undermine their drive to innovate. Many talented Black women in higher learning ultimately find themselves in a lonely place due to fear of rejection (Porter et al. 2020; Hinton 2010; Patitu and Hinton 2003). It is critical to mention that Black women do not enter academia expecting rejection, especially in spaces that, on the surface, seem to represent, embrace, and empower them. Regardless of the institution, the subjective path toward tenure and promotion is all too similar to hazing.

Black women in academia are not immune or insulated from the social constructs and stereotypes of Black femininity. They persist in mainstream media, other social arenas, and experiences common to Black women, overall. In the context of this chapter, these constructs also prevail in higher education. They are both internalized and inflicted to contribute to the ongoing oppression of Black female academics (Harris-Perry 2011; Patton and Haynes 2018; Haynes et al. 2020). Personified, these cultural stereotypes include the *Superwoman*, *Troublemaker*, and *Protector*, which the authors explore through the lived experiences of Black female HBCU faculty, whose collective identities are represented through the use of three pseudonyms: Clarke, Cookie, and Keisha, respectively.

CLARKE: I'M EVERY WOMAN

> If I was paid five dollars for every time a colleague told me, "I don't know how you do it," I'd be paid my worth in academia!

Clarke represents the superwomen, the gladiators who, based on their stellar skills and reputation, are called when excellence is required and crises need to be *handled* in academic spaces. Many publicly revere, lean heavily on, and—arguably—exploit Clarke's strengths to support the needs of students, fellow colleagues, and the success of the institution itself. They are Swiss army knives and perceived, accurately, to do a variety of things—big and small—well. The resourcefulness, diverse skills, and servant-leader personas make many Black female academics the perennial go-to for tasks, projects, and leadership positions. However, far too often, when it comes to evaluation, the same traits that make Clarkes an invaluable asset are suddenly liabilities. This superwoman strength is weaponized.

My direct supervisors knew full well the significance of their words and their glaring omissions in my performance evaluation. They were uniquely positioned to celebrate my less visible wins—the multiple hats I wore, opportunities I created, positive changes I facilitated at various levels. Their sparse statements and recommendation for me to limit my university activities was a veiled suggestion that my highly visible role was to blame—not the 55 hats I was routinely asked to wear, gaps I was implored to fill for inactive colleagues, roles that persisted despite my repeated request for reprieve. That neither supervisor acknowledged that the biggest threats to my research and scholarship were the things they routinely asked of me was mind numbing. It was confusing. I never saw my "mentors" the same way after that. How could I?

As another Clarke conveys, being a Jill-of-all-trades meant that she was tapped to do "extracurricular" things (e.g., support tech-challenged colleagues, serve on special committees, pinch-hit on administrator tasks, and adopt excessive academic advisees). Clarkes' plates are perpetually full. While feeling needed and impactful satiates their altruistic nature, as tenure-track educators, most Clarkes do not feel that saying "no" is a viable option.

However, as resourceful and resilient as most Clarkes are, superheroes cannot be everywhere or everything to everyone. Even when Clarkes are able to succeed at keeping all balls in the air, this talent is not always respected and, in fact, is sometimes resented. This sentiment is rarely expressed overtly, however; it comes out in passive-aggressive ways, such as a combined praise-and-pitch sandwich, which usually begins with "I know your plate is full, but . . ." while adding more demands to their plates. It also manifests as seeds of doubt planted in private, such as in written evaluations.

I cannot fully articulate the gut punch I felt when I reviewed the ratings included in my annual evaluation. The overall chair ratings were noticeably lower than my self-ratings. The irony was that I had finally embraced my Black Girl Magic and gave myself the ratings I deserved (unlike previous years where my peers and mentor told me that I was not giving myself enough credit). The 63 glared back at me like a D on a transcript. That I rated myself as 73 in the same category implied that either I overvalued my worth or that my chair sees me as having deficiencies in the areas that count most for promotion in rank. Thinking about the impression this would make on each of the tenure and promotion review committees made me ill. Knowing that my chair also knew the weight this would have on my dossier made me feel angry . . . and set up to be rejected. It felt exceedingly personal, painful, and petty.

COOKIE: ACADEMIC ABANDONMENT

I regret not standing firm in my decision to move forward and let them tell me "no"!

Cookie's promotion story is one of misplaced trust in her department "family" that led to personal and professional estrangement. The Cookies of academia enter HBCUs eager and excited. Their impressive level of productivity—submitting publications for consecutive years, receiving excellent teaching evaluations, serving on multiple committees—more than qualify them for tenure with promotion in rank.

However, the Cookies of academia are rarely rewarded for exceeding criteria. Often, Cookies earn tenure but are denied the simultaneous promotion they deserve. As one Cookie testifies, she was denied promotion by her department and college-level committees yet supported for both tenure and promotion at the university-committee level. The administrative gatekeepers ultimately justified their recommendation to deny her promotion by deferring to Cookie's department colleagues, whom they alleged "knew [her] best." When Cookie later asked for justification of her denied promotion, two senior tenured faculty in her department proclaimed, "That's the way it has *always* been. *We* did not get tenure and promotion when we went up [for both]."

This generational practice and the subsequent public rejection was deflating, and Cookie did not reapply for promotion for several years. By then, the timeline for several publications that once overqualified Cookie for promotion had expired and thus could no longer be considered for evaluation. Consequently, Cookie produced additional research over the next couple of years to ensure her eligibility to reapply.

To add insult to injury, an ill-timed technicality led to Cookie's dossier being denied a second time; without the publisher's written confirmation that her chapter would be published shortly after the dossier submission deadline, the powers-that-be followed the recommendation of the university committee that Cookie wait another year. No one else seemed bothered by this cavalier suggestion for Cookie to put her career on hold. Fortunately, at long last, she finally prevailed the following year.

As Cookie prepared her dossier for promotion to full professor, she felt that there was something different about this time. Cookie had grown to trust her colleagues in the department. She had finally found her intellectual home and felt like part of the family. Even colleagues who relied on long-held traditions now felt like allies. Cookie gave herself permission to exhale! But when a series of events led to her decision to rescind her application, this failed attempt hurt personally and professionally. In hindsight, Cookie acknowledged that by letting down her guard, she entrusted her career to her colleagues, especially her department head and confidant, "Peter." She naively assumed that her colleagues were equally invested in her promotion, as her success was a reflection of the department's success. Sadly, she was mistaken.

Cookie did not retreat, nor did she hide her feelings of defeat. This time, Cookie would get into *good trouble*. Unlike years prior, Cookie asserted herself and called out Peter for his inaction on behalf of her success in her well-deserved promotion. Although Peter conveyed regret, and even acknowledged some ownership for the oversight that cost Cookie a promotion, Peter was all too resigned about not accepting solutions. Despite being presented with a collaborative scholarly opportunity that would not only secure Cookie's eligibility but also concurrently provide an avenue to ameliorate Peter's oversight, he instead distanced himself.

Although disappointed, Cookie felt resolute in her decision to move forward and let the committee tell her "no"—her record of excellence was evident, and Peter was in a position to champion her by highlighting her accomplishments in total. However, Peter's persistent revisiting of Cookie's decision to move forward ultimately undermined Cookie's confidence in Peter's sponsorship. It was implied that the regret he expressed and ownership for this precarious position was a sufficient show of his support and, more importantly, Cookie should simply accept the situation and wait to reapply. This time, for Cookie, it was

Peter's resignation about her fate that she found most disheartening. Reluctantly, she acquiesced, attempting to avoid alienation, but feelings of alienation ultimately manifested.

> Even if Peter's efforts to resolve the oversight had failed, knowing that he had sponsored me to the end of the process would have made a world of difference. His sponsorship would have eliminated feelings of deflation and feelings of mistrust.

Peter is symbolic of alleged colleagues who engage in performative praise but endeavor to strategically control Black women, such that they *appear* to be solely responsible for undermining their own success. At times, such tactics are tantamount to gaslighting and ultimately result in Black female faculty apologizing for things over which they never had control. In this case, we see that Cookie ultimately found herself apologizing to Peter to keep the peace. While peacekeeping can be a noble effort, it releases the Peters of the world from accountability for their damaging decisions while continuing to treat the Cookies of academia as if they were at fault all along. Black women rarely call out the Peters of the world for fear of being abandoned altogether. Yet, as in Cookie's situation, that was the end result, despite her best defenses.

> We don't want to be seen as whiners, troublemakers, or persistent complainers. "There she goes again!" So, then we go on mute! Then our careers go stagnant. Our light, once bright, goes dim.

Black faculty have enough experience of navigating predominately White spaces to remain vigilant against the inevitable battle of "educating while Black" (Daut 2019; Lee and Leonard 2001). At an HBCU, there is not only a sense of cultural pride but also a disarming sense of belongingness (Leslie et al. 2021; Sessoms, Lynch, and Edmonds 2021). Black faculty navigate without the weight of the emotional and intellectual armor and the fatigue of maintaining a persistent defensive position, because it seems unnecessary, even unfathomable, in such a welcoming space.

However, feeling at ease and assuming the space is safe may be costly and, the authors argue, may subject Black faculty to exploitation. Many Black academics have learned that all faculty are not employed at HBCUs for the same reasons or motives, nor do they apply the same values toward the legacy, mission, or scholars of these cultural institutions of higher learning. As the narratives of several Black female faculty at HBCUs suggest, some of the most insidious indignities have been at the hands of fellow colleagues of color, such as the toxic generational practices of not granting simultaneous tenure and promotion (Edmonds 2021). These have been painful reminders that "all skinfolk ain't kinfolk."

KEISHA: STRENGTH IN NUMBERS

> There's something special about a woman who dominates in a man's world. It takes a certain grace, strength, intelligence, fearlessness, and the nerve to never take no for an answer. —Rihanna (quoted in Vivanco and Ottenburg 2017)

Keisha was fortunate to have the protective role of sponsorship modeled for her by two strong women of color, "Colleen" and "Naomi," who served on her dissertation committee. These women held the line against her two male committee counterparts when they told Keisha that her dissertation needed more work—specifically, "more pages"— although she and the rest of her committee deemed her dissertation complete. This is a prime example of sisterhood in the academy, which the authors posit, should be the norm, rather than the exception.

However, the reality is that Black female faculty are often left to wonder who holds the line for them. The authors attest that this is precisely what is required: a call to arms for Black women faculty—the Colleens and Naomis of the world—to close ranks, hold the line for each other when oppressors try to demote, deny, and defame them. Black women are called to show up in their role as sponsors when they are seated at the table. Rather than worry about risking their place in the gated community and placating others to ensure that they keep it, Black female faculty must boldly bring other women to the table. There is strength in numbers and fortitude in solidarity with our sisters in the academy.

To clarify, the Clarkes and Cookies of the world have not been without mentors throughout their journey in academia. However, far too often, those who are positioned and perceived as standing in the gap for Black female faculty indeed widen this gap by failing to speak up—and speak out—on behalf of their sisters. These mentors are uniquely positioned to empower and elevate fellow Black female colleagues, yet some continue to fear risking their positions or perceived power and, consequently, do a disservice to themselves and their colleagues by remaining silent when their sisters' fates are being sealed. This is true at PWIs and HBCUs.

Mentoring and sponsorship are paramount for Black women in the academy (Jernigan, Dudley, and Hatch 2020). Regardless of institution, Black female academics are perceived as threats from every angle and, consequently, experience pushback from several sectors—self-serving White faculty, egocentric Black men, White women ever-ready to play damsels in distress, and some students who devalue them as *othermothers*. At HBCUs, academic violence (Gillians and Cooper 2021) comes from microaggressions, such as colleagues who marvel, "You're so good at _____. You're so strong!" coupled with amazement over how many tasks Black female colleagues manage, yet the same individuals do nothing to lighten these heavy loads. Frequently, such comments are followed by additional *asks* for assistance as colleagues assume that the work *they* were personally tasked to do can be added on top of already-overflowing plates.

Even when some Black men feign support as public allies who claim to know and understand "the struggle," they are still unwilling to use their positions and power to secure that of a Black female colleague. This is evident in lamentations about growing tired of hearing about the genuine struggle Black women experience in academia, and issuing warnings about hearing them "whine." *So what do we do?* Not only do we stop whining, but we also stop talking altogether and become selectively mute. Black women in the academy know all too well why the caged bird sings.

While it is not uncommon for men and women in the academy to have different experiences and approaches, solidarity among female faculty is not necessarily the norm. Some of our fellow sisters in higher education are also complicit by staying silent in the situation room, for fear of being the center of their own "situation" or placing their allegiances to other affinities, regional and organizational, above the good of the larger sisterhood. With few Black males to speak on behalf of all Black experiences, fewer White women to use their voices as feminists, and rarely a sister among them willing to risk the perception of being an agitator or the recipient of unmerited favor, Black women are often left sponsorless behind closed doors, orphaned in their departments and homeless during homecoming at their HBCUs. Thus, when asked, "Is there one among you . . . ?" and commanded to "speak now or forever hold your peace," the silence is deafening.

WATCHING AND WAITING TO EXHALE

So what does it mean for Black female HBCU faculty to continue "watching and waiting to exhale"? How do we ensure the affirmation and ascension of Black women in academia? The authors contend that it starts with being armed with intelligence and spiritual armor: "Be alert and sober of mind" (I Peter 5:8 NIV). Watching means being vigilant and understanding, as a result of communing with sisters and learning the secret sauce—the tricks of the enemy. Black female academics must rely on the brilliant blueprint of their ancestors, who survived the ultimate subjugation of slavery.

Black women in the academy must use the intel that they gain from leadership positions, other roles, relationships, and places to bring back to the secret gathering spots. They must connect with trusted allies to collect tips on how to avoid pitfalls and bait-and-switch schemes, and relay covert messages across the sisterhood through drumming, hymns, and yard songs.

EMBRACE THE MARGINS

As Hill Collins (2000) underscores, the Black American womanhood collective identity has evolved from the tension of the oppression and resistance we have experienced over our lifetime. This speaks to the significance of affinity groups—safe spaces and places for us to share our journeys, dispense wisdom, express our exasperations, and empower one another to exploit the margins for our collective benefit (Hill Collins 2000; hooks 2000).

Contrary to the perception of HBCUs as feeling like home and a family for students and faculty of color (Leslie et al. 2021), these narratives underscore the imperative need for Black women in the academy to have physical, emotional, and communal spaces to share and process their experiences. Affinity groups must transcend commiseration and catharsis. Black women in higher education must be intentional about providing training, restoring trust in mentoring, and exchanging success stories and pages from the oppressors' playbooks that they glean from navigating other spaces. Black women must use the margins as their underground railroad to mobilize.

TELL YOUR STORY AND LET THEM TELL YOU NO

Black women vocalizing their experiences are bona fide acts of resistance. It is hard, but necessary, to acknowledge Black women's stories and name their pain privately and publicly, to themselves first and then to other Black women. These exploits are critical to articulate and disperse because these stories, the authors now realize, were never for others anyway. As the authors learned through this journey, breaking silence is therapeutic. Black women's stories must be publicly expressed in order to provide historical markers for the next generation of women embracing their Black excellence. Further, interrogating them among each other will remind each subsequent generation how imperative it is to continue this legacy.

Black women in the academy, in particular, need to share their narratives in scholarly discourse, and continually affirm that doing so is, indeed, scholarly in nature, history, and deed. As effective epistemology reminds us, our lived experiences are valued ways of knowing (Schiele 2013). While academic spaces have historically invalidated their narrative, Black feminist thought contends that the expression of Black women's personal journeys should be regarded as a critical social theory (Alinia 2015). Accordingly, in order for their experiences to be regarded as scholarly, Black women faculty must first embrace it as valid, significant, and worthy.

The Clarkes, Cookies, and Keishas represented here were bold enough to allow us to publicly share their journeys. The authors cannot underscore how challenging, emotional, and courageous it was to do so. Offering these narratives was not without trepidation, as they feared their oppressors might recognize themselves in their testimonies. However, the authors and contributors collectively recognized that they needed and deserved this release and redemption, as "nothing can be changed until it is faced" (Baldwin 1962). Through their testimonies, each reclaimed and raised her voice. Moreover, this endeavor amplifies the necessity to model the very state of being unbothered by reactions of any oppressors, as the authors are encouraging their sisters reading this chapter to be.

Also, the authors recognize that this trepidation is the manifestation of deeply internalized oppression felt by Black women in the academy and the subsequent conditioned state of silence that they sustained to their own detriment. However, as scholars and subject matter experts in mental health, the authors affirm that what has been conditioned can also be counter-conditioned—unlearned, unraveled, unbound! *Give us free!* This liberation starts with recognizing the state of learned helplessness in which Black female faculty have been mired—and it continues with intentional efforts to disentangle mental associations of struggle and strife with minds and life experiences of Black women in academia.

BECOME UNBOTHERED—I SAID WHAT I SAID

Speaking up in sacred and public spaces is also necessary for self-preservation—Black women must shift their protection to themselves. History has proven that no one will protect Black women in the academy; no one will cover them, so they must cover themselves—and each other—and be unburdened about being perceived as disruptors. Moreover, Black women must not be troubled by how oppressors and obstructionists will receive or process their truths—they must learn to be and *remain* unbothered by the discomfort it will elicit in others. Black women in higher education must practice calling *out* oppressors and calling *in* complicit colleagues alike—diplomatically, yet publicly! Black women in the academy must embrace the freedom of deciding how and when they show up—and *not* apologize for how they do so, especially at an HBCU!

CLOSE RANKS

When Black women support one another, they are an unmatched force. In the film rendition of Alice Walker's *The Color Purple* (Spielberg 1985), Sophia's sisters consistently make their unspoken yet unwavering support known and immediately close ranks around her at the mere hint of foul play. Once Black women discern their kindred spirits in the academy, they must be willing to flow the same way—celebrate each other's milestones, but also be willing to get in formation. This sisterhood includes peers, mentors, sponsors, and elders. Black women in the academy closing ranks also means not falling for age-old tricks used against them and, instead, mastering how and when to dismantle them. Finally, Black female faculty need to be ready to help their sister pack up her belongings and leave where she is not valued.

SIT IN YOUR SEAT OF HONOR

Even when Black female faculty do not have a seat at the table, they must be reminded that wherever they sit—in the mainstream or in the margins—it is a well-earned seat of honor. Allow the authors to take the liberty to speak directly to fellow Black women in the academy:
Give yourselves permission to embrace your humanity and hold up a mirror so your sister can see hers, too! As these narratives have illustrated—if not *you*, then who? As Black female academics, you will never be seen as whole women with full plates and fuller lives on and off campus until you believe this yourself. Moreover, until you believe that Black women in the academy, too, are equally—if not more—deserving of reprieve and restoration as our colleagues are, you will actively reinforce, rather than realign, your boundaries.

Sister scholars, your strength is in your self-preservation, and your resistance is in the reclamation of your time and peace of mind. Simply stating that your schedule is "fully committed" is more than sufficient. Resisting the urge to explain yourself or redirect the inquiry is also a quiet, revolutionary act. Why? *Because I said what I said!*

Finally, if you must be *Superwomen*, use your powers for your own good and that of the sisterhood. Use affinity spaces for more than commiseration; use them instead for collaboration—in scholarship, service, spirituality, and socialization. When you see your sisters in the academy falling into old patterns, you absolutely must call her *in* and counsel her (Ross 2019). As reflected in this chapter, and the entire edited volume that you now hold in your hands, you must invite others to these sacred sister circles to continue critically examining your experiences and use it to expand your minds and leverage your opportunities. When necessary, the strength of the sisterhood could also be mobilized to call out injustices, large and small, politically and, if necessary, legally. Finally, the sisterhood should also rally in support of those who grow weary of battle fatigue and choose to take their talents elsewhere, including outside of academia.

Akin to what Claude McKay's poem "If We Must Die" emboldens the reader to consider, if Black women in the academy must be protectors, they should be sentinels of the sisterhood. If Black women must be sheroes, they should reserve their capes and compassion to avail themselves, and work together as avengers of the collective. Likewise, Black women faculty must reject attempts by the oppressor to regard their strengths as kryptonite to deny deserved opportunities. Instead, they must convert these assets into cryptocurrency to pay the poll tax demanded to enter the guarded and gated community of academia.

Space does not permit the authors to tell every sister's story. There are far more Clarkes, Cookies, and Keishas in our midst. Moreover, there is not sufficient room to offer more recommendations to ensure the personal and professional survival of fellow sister scholars. It is the authors' genuine aspiration that this chapter has magnified the visibility and amplified the full humanity of Black female faculty and, in so doing, inspired you, the reader, to extend the conversation of this pivotal work.

REFERENCES

Alinia, Minoo. 2015. "On *Black Feminist Thought*: Thinking Oppression and Resistance through Intersectional Paradigm." *Ethnic and Racial Studies* 38, no. 13: 2334–40.
Baldwin, James. 1962, January 14. "As Much Truth as One Can Bear." *New York Times*, Book Review Section, p. BR38.

Carter, TaLisa J., and Miltonette O. Craig. 2022, March. "It Could Be Us: Black Faculty as 'Threats' on the Path to Tenure." *Race and Justice.*

Collins, Patricia Hill. 2000. *Black Feminist Thought.* 2nd ed. New York: Routledge.

Crenshaw, Kimberlé W. 2017. *On Intersectionality: Essential Writings.* New York: The New Press.

Daut, Marlene L. 2019. "Becoming Full Professor while Black." *The Chronicle of Higher Education* 28.

del Priore, Andrea. 2022. "Strategies for Support: Black Women Faculty Career Advancement at Historically Black Colleges and Universities." *Journal of Black Studies* 53, no. 1: 19–44.

Edmonds, Wendy M. 2021. *InTOXICating Followership: In the Jonestown Massacre.* Bingley, UK: Emerald.

Gillians, Phyllis E., and Bruce S. Cooper. 2021. *Keeping School Children Safe and Alive: Strategies to Stop Bullying and Prevent Suicide.* Charlotte, NC: Information Age.

Harris-Perry, Melissa V. 2011. *Sister Citizen: Shame, Stereotypes, and Black Women in America.* New Haven, CT: Yale University Press.

Haynes, Chayla, Leonard Taylor, Steve D. Mobley Jr, and Jasmine Haywood. 2020. "Existing and Resisting: The Pedagogical Realities of Black, Critical Men and Women Faculty." *The Journal of Higher Education* 91, no. 5: 698–721.

Hinton, Dawn. 2010. "Creating Community on the Margins: The Successful Black Female Academician." *Urban Rev* 42, 394–402.

hooks, bell. 1989. *Talking Back: Thinking Feminist, Thinking Black.* Boston: South End Press.

hooks, bell. 2000. *Feminist Theory: From Margin to Center.* London: Pluto Press.

Jernigan, Quintara A., Manuel C. Dudley, and Bryle Henderson Hatch. 2020. "Mentoring Matters: Experiences in Mentoring Black Leaders in Higher Education." *New Directions for Adult and Continuing Education,* no. 167–68 (Fall/Winter): 43–57.

Lee, Laura J., and Curtis A. Leonard. 2001. "Violence in Predominantly White Institutions of Higher Education: Tenure and Victim Blaming." *Journal of Human Behavior in the Social Environment* 4, no. 2–3: 167–86.

Leslie, Annie Ruth, Kim Brittingham Barnett, Matasha L. Harris, and Charles Adams. 2021. "Advancing the Demarginalization of African American Students." In *The Black Experience and Navigating Higher Education Through a Virtual World,* edited by Kimetta R. Hairston, Wendy M. Edmonds, and Shanetia P. Clark, 73–96. Hershey, PA: IGI Global.

Lorde, Audre. 2020. *The Selected Works of Audre Lorde*. New York: W. W. Norton.

Patitu, Carol Logan, and Kandace G. Hinton. 2003. "The Experiences of African American Women Faculty and Administrators in Higher Education: Has Anything Changed?" *New Directions for Student Services* 2003, no. 104: 79–93.

Patton, L. D., and C. Haynes. 2018. "Hidden in Plain Sight: The Black Women's Blueprint for Institutional Transformation in Higher Education." *Teachers College Record* 120, no. 4: 1–18.

Porter, Christa J., Candace M. Moore, Ginny J. Boss, Tiffany J. Davis, and Dave A. Louis. 2020. "To Be Black Women and Contingent Faculty: Four Scholarly Personal Narratives." *The Journal of Higher Education* 91, no. 5: 674–97.

Ross, Loretta. 2019, August 17. "I'm a Black Feminist. I Think Call-Out Culture Is Toxic." *New York Times*. www.nytimes.com/2019/08/17/opinion/sunday/cancel-culture-call-out.html.

Schiele, Jerome H. *Human Services and the Afrocentric Paradigm*. New York: Routledge, 2013.

Sessoms, Diallo, Ayanna M. Lynch, and Wendy M. Edmonds. 2021."Beyond Social Distance: The Cultural and Digital Divide at an HBCU." In *The Black Experience and Navigating Higher Education through a Virtual World*, edited by Kimetta R. Hairston, Wendy M. Edmonds, and Shanetia P. Clark, 39–52. Hershey, PA: IGI Global.

Sinclair-Chapman, Valeria. 2019. "Rebounding on the Tenure Track: Carving Out a Place of Your Own in the Academy." *PS: Political Science & Politics* 52, no. 1: 52–56.

Spielberg, Steven, dir. 1985. *The Color Purple*. Burbank, CA: Warner Bros. DVD.

Vivanco, Mariono, and Mel Ottenburg. 2017, February 8. "Rihanna Takes Flight." *Harper's Bazaar*. www.harpersbazaar.com/culture/features/a20446/rihanna-amelia-earhart-photo-shoot.

CHAPTER 2

From Underdog to Accomplished
Persevering through Unexpected Challenges
Nina Jacks

Don't sit down and wait for the opportunities to come. Get up and make them. —Madam C. J. Walker

Rashida's story is one of success. She was told that she could graduate with a doctorate degree within three years, and Rashida did it! The hope is that women of color will read this and be encouraged to persevere through any barrier and know that this goal is attainable. Rashida's doctoral journey was multilayered, and this chapter explores the program practices, academic and social support, impacts of COVID-19, and lessons learned from this life-changing experience.

According to Merriam-Webster (n.d.), an underdog is a loser or predicted loser in a struggle or contest, a victim of injustice or persecution. For women of color, this can often be the reality. Thus, the first challenge that Rashida overcame was the feeling of being an underdog because she was not an administrator like most of her cohort members. Corley (2020) posits that women of color who experience the intersectionality of race and gender bias frequently display a superior work ethic than their White counterparts to prove themselves more because women of color are subjected to unequal standards.

Despite studies reporting that the retention and completion at the doctoral level for women of color remain issues to be addressed, the National Center for Education Statistics (2020) shows that women of color have made significant progress in completing college at higher rates and obtaining advanced degrees than in the past. Comparatively, Patterson-Stephens and Hernández (2018) report that there is an existing gap in extant literature that tells the stories of Black, Indigenous,

Latina, and Asian women. More specifically, the lived experiences of women of color in doctoral programs are seldom explored.

It is further documented that academia's culture of competition and individualism (Patterson-Stephens and Hernández 2018) often make women of color feel marginalized and experience feelings of inferiority. This was not always the case in Rashida's experience. Her doctoral cohort consisted of working adults and one full-time student. As a result, the cohort members were all too busy to be competitive, most of the time.

During the first semester of classes, the cohort members regularly came together to discuss assignments and offer suggestions of resources and strategies. They congratulated and celebrated each other's accomplishments and encouraged persistence to graduation. As previously stated, Rashida's feelings of inadequacy during the first few classes were a result of not having administrative experiences like her colleagues, who were principals and assistant principals. Rashida knew she possessed knowledge and expertise she could offer, but her contributions were of a different context. However, once Rashida affirmed for herself that she belonged, she never looked back. In fact, Rashida was one of two in the cohort who graduated with a doctorate on time.

Further, Corley's (2020) assertion that, historically, women have struggled to capture leadership positions in most industries was also not true in Rashida's situation. She works in a school system that is dominated by women and that employs women of color in leadership roles (Prince George's County Public Schools, n.d.). Consequently, Rashida has a Black female mentor who is secure in her professional life and therefore offers Rashida opportunities to grow and excel in her profession as well.

To achieve academic and professional success, you must be knowledgeable within your academic field, make sense of the campus community, and feel empowered to use your voice regardless of whether or not you are in a White space or accompanied by colleagues who look like you. Program policies and practices often determine the level of equity and access based on gender and/or race (Young and Anderson 2021). Thank God Rashida knew how to navigate these gates.

PROGRAM PRACTICES

Another unexpected challenge Rashida quickly overcame was accepting that a Historically Black College or University (HBCU) would appoint a White male as her doctoral program advisor. In fact, the presence of other White faculty and students at an HBCU (see table 2.1) was a program practice that required a social adjustment for Rashida. However, after three years of working alongside White faculty and students, Rashida's perspective shifted, and she partially agrees with the U.S. Supreme Court (in *Fisher v. University of Texas* 2016) that creating diverse racial climates on college campuses enhances the broad educational mission of higher-education institutions by exposing students to new perspectives. Thus, interactions with other races can *sometimes* improve students' skills and prepare them to better serve their community as qualified workers and leaders.

Accordingly, Davis, Reese, and Griswold (2020) report that women of color feel that their presence in a diverse program and their participation in class discussions and activities contribute to their classmates' understanding of a broader spectrum and nuance in Black experience than is typically portrayed in the media and that is often perpetuated as negative or less than their White counterparts. One Black female shares:

I've been accepted as I am. I don't have to change my language, my tone and again it's professional. I can be Black and be professional. I can be Black, and I can be educated. I can be Black and articulate. I can be Black and have a critical or controversial conversation. I can have

Table 2.1. Description of University Faculty

Race/Ethnicity	Gender	Faculty Position
White	male	associate professor/program director
White	male	assistant professor
White	female	adjunct professor
Black	female	adjunct professor
White	male	adjunct professor
Black	female	assistant professor
Black	male	adjunct professor
Black	female	adjunct professor

a difficult discussion and still be Black and not be aggressive but still assertive. Does that come with my Blackness? I don't know. (210)

Rashida did not see a Black professor until the second semester of classes. As a graduate of a prominent HBCU, Rashida had never had a White professor or any White students in her classes. She knew others in the cohort who looked like her felt at times they had to minimize their Blackness because of the White colleagues in the room. Although the cohort members did have some honest conversations, Rashida was convinced the dialogue would have been different if the Black students were in an all-Black space.

Why do Black women feel as if they must silence or tone down their contributions when White people are present? This made Rashida think about the vice-presidential debate on October 6, 2020, which demonstrated how Senator Kamala Harris "held back" more than she did in previous debates. Rashida wondered what the results would have been if all the students and professors had been Black. Would the discussions have been more relevant? Would the students in the cohort have tried harder to graduate on time? Would the expectations have been higher?

At times, the diversity of the cohort (see table 2.2) was highlighted, but it never affected Rashida's confidence in bringing perspectives and experiences to class discussions. This reality can be juxtaposed with

Table 2.2. Racial, Gender, and Professional Demographics of Rashida's Doctoral Cohort

Race/Ethnicity	Gender	Position/Title
Black	female	principal
Black	female	assistant principal
Black	female	assistant principal
Black	female	assistant principal
Black	female	instructional coach
Black	female	instructional coach
White	female	central office administrator
White	female	principal
White	female	instructional coach
White	male	retired teacher
Black	male	full-time student
Black	female	assistant principal
Black	female	instructional coach

research from Davis et al. (2020), who report that the use of humor in classes often served to deflect potentially uncomfortable comments. This humor may have also kept discussions of "racially charged and/or gendered issues" (209) safely unapproachable and possibly unaddressed.

Comparatively, Rashid's cohort did discuss racially charged issues. She remembered one of her colleagues lamenting about how exhausting it was having to play innocent or unaffected by ignorant comments and microaggressions implied by two White female professors. Rashida remembered one professor treating the non-administrators and non-White students as if they had nothing to contribute to the discussions. This professor consistently called on one White principal to respond to questions and stated, "You know everything—you're a principal."

The Black students shared a look of incredulousness as they stared at each other and shook their heads. The other Black principal mumbled, "I'm a principal too." Rashida also remembered feeling invisible. A few students laughed at the audacity, but this was only the second course as a cohort, and Rashida believed the students were all feeling each other out, establishing allies, and creating rapports.

Davis et al. (2020) posit that, although for the most part, Black participants did not describe racial microaggressions that they had experienced in interactions with faculty, there were a few incidents. "One such incident involved a faculty member who did not remember students' names" (209). Similarly, this White female professor that Rashida had ignorantly associated two colleagues of Caribbean backgrounds as the same. Some students shared where they were born and their ethnicities; during another class the professor stated, "[Student A] is from Jamaica." This was incorrect because Student A's family was from a country in South America, but Student A was born in the United States and was mistaken or associated with another student from Jamaica. When the students corrected the professor, she waved her hand and said, "Well yeah, they weren't born here."

The obvious connection among the Black students was that they were the same race and thus understood what was happening. The problem was the Black students were not vested enough after just one month to take a stand. Some colleagues discussed the incident during the breaks and after class, but no one really addressed what took place. The Black students were probably as used to microaggressions as Rashida, but the blatant disregard for the other students who earned their acceptance to the doctoral program was alarming.

The second White female professor, with positive intentions, revised the content of one class to highlight White allies. The professor showed the cohort a TED Talk where a Black woman reminisced about a White teacher who she referred to as her "hero" because the White teacher took an interest in the Black woman's life. Further, this White professor went on to share her difficult childhood struggles as a poor White girl. Rashida remembered being confused and unable to relate; it was almost as if the professor assumed that all Blacks would understand because all Blacks struggle too, right?

The major difference here was that this encounter took place toward the end of the cohort's second year. Students were more vocal and addressed the issue. The professor apologized and explained that she was trying to show that there were White allies ready and willing to support Blacks and that some White people grew up like Blacks so they could share their successes as an incentive to motivate others to succeed. The ignorant reasoning prompted Rashida to share her upbringing and childhood experiences. She simply told the cohort, "I grew up with a maid and a cook. My parents paid cash for my college tuition and siblings' tuition." Do not put Black people in a box! Do not assume all Blacks have the same experiences!

Sadly, there appears to be a misconception that Blacks all have the same upbringing, and all are from the same socioeconomic situation. Participants in Davis et al.'s (2020) study counter this notion: the study represents a breadth of Blackness that some White peers in their cohort were not privy to. Many of the Black participants are third- or fourth-generation college graduates and come from prosperous backgrounds. Black scholars have varied backgrounds, but White peers may not realize this. Accordingly, the counter-narrative in Davis et al.'s (2020) study is defined by an asset background that promoted student confidence and agency. One participant states:

> So interestingly enough, the African Americans that were in the program were not first generation, were not low income, weren't what they expected. They expected us to be the low income, the first generation.

We were all middle class. We all came from educated backgrounds. . . .
So they had different expectations of who we were. . . . And I said,
"We're the opposite of what you think we're supposed to be." (210)

Although Davis et al.'s (2020) participants provide narratives that
note barriers including microaggressions and intermittent feelings of
inadequacy, the study highlights the varied success and experience
as leaders in participants' respective workplaces and home communities. Similarly, Davis et al. (2020) have found that perceptions of
the cohort's openness to and respect for the contributions of African
American students varies with different cohorts. Comparatively, Black
female students have shared that their initial reservations as African
Americans in their doctoral program did not come to fruition. Instead,
these women have found that "the vibe" (208) was positive and com-
pletely different from previous negative experiences.

Overall, the White participants in Rashida's cohort mentioned how
being in the cohort with Black professionals allowed them to learn
more about Blacks in general. The White students shared how they
tried to provide equity and access in their respective roles as administrators and educators of Black students. Similarly, Davis et al. (2020)
report that although some of the graduates of doctoral programs
develop an interest in pursuing faculty positions in higher education,
a significant number of educators are motivated to pursue leadership
positions where they can positively impact educational issues in the
urban environments in which most work. Further, these recent graduates take advantage of the support and insights developed through participation with diverse peers.

ACADEMIC AND SOCIAL SUPPORT: UNEXPECTED ALLIES

Rashida was thankful that her White male advisor, and eventually dissertation chair, was welcoming from their first conversation. He was
helpful, straightforward, and obviously had experience guiding adults
through the program. This retired public-school superintendent provided the big picture of the doctoral program and laid out expectations
from the first Friday evening class. The program was well designed and
provided step-by-step support toward degree completion.

Rashida was provided a timeline, she was afforded the opportunity to become published in an academic journal, her required internship transitioned into a full-time assignment in the form of a job promotion, and every course offered the potential to gather information toward Rashida's dissertation topic. The most valuable advice given by her advisor was to "write for one hour every day." This suggestion was significant and impacted Rashida's successful completion of her doctorate degree. This White male fully supported every student regardless of race.

Initially, Rashida had great expectations of her Black cohort members. She believed that they would all be on the same academic level and support each other with assignments and activities. This was not the case. On the surface, the cohort worked well together. However, that is where the relationships ended. As working adults, each led their own lives during the week, and then the members would convene on the weekends for the doctoral program. On the contrary, Rashida joined the program with a Black female colleague. They roomed together each weekend, shared ideas, and offered advice on each other's work products; they laughed, cried, prayed, and excelled through the program. Social and academic support for these two was reciprocated during the first two years of coursework.

Rashida mastered the plan: write for one hour each day. By the time students were expected to submit a proposal defense and progress to the Internal Review Board (IRB), Rashida was one of two students who were ready. The other prepared student was a White woman from Rashida's cohort. Sure, they saw each other on weekends, they listened to each other's contributions during class discussions, and they even chatted occasionally since they were often the two early birds. Because the dissertation process is linear, Rashida's Black colleagues were now a few paces behind her, and she had no one with whom she could connect academically.

As a result, the only other person in Rashida's cohort who was on track for graduation was a White female. Naturally, she and Rashida began to check in more often and share information about the writing and research process. They provided one another with mutual support and guidance as they progressed through the program. Davis et al. (2020) posit that cohorts are increasingly a significant factor in doctoral programs and cultures. In fact, cohorts may splinter into cliques and will certainly encounter tensions regarding social issues. These characteristics describe Rashida's cohort during the second year of coursework. However, Davis et al. (2020) also report that the effects of the cohort model were generally positive and had the potential to offer a sense of community.

Comparatively, Corley (2020) reports that women of color often feel isolated because there are few in their respective fields. This isolation often led to a lack of social engagement, which was seen as necessary for academic and personal success. This was not the case for Rashida. On the contrary, social isolation was a welcomed default toward the end of the program because of the COVID-19 pandemic. Rashida was able to focus. She learned her worth as a professional and a doctoral student. She discovered her potential and capabilities, and Rashida knew that she would graduate on time. Thus, her need for academic support shifted to feedback on the final two dissertation chapters. Social support came in the form of healthy competition and an overwhelming need to prove that Rashida was just as good as, if not better than, her White counterparts.

Ironically, Rashida learned more about the history of Black people during her two years of research than she did in all her years of public school. Rashida was angry as she read about the miseducation she was taught, the systemic racism of the United States, and when Rashida could not find enough positive literature to counterbalance the degrading accounts of people who looked like her Black husband and Black son, she knew she had to complete her dissertation. Adding to the "body of knowledge" was no longer just a partial requirement for Rashida's degree; it was a necessity for other Black students who were searching for literature to validate what Rashida already knew to be true: there *are* Black people with college degrees.

During her final year, Rashida had three allies who did not look like her: Rashida's advisor was an older White male, her original dissertation chair was an older White male, and the cohort member with whom Rashida had the most in common during the dissertation process was a White woman.

NAVIGATING THE UNKNOWN THROUGH THE
COVID-19 PANDEMIC

What began as a traditional higher-learning experience in a brick-and-mortar setting abruptly shifted, along with the rest of the world, to an unknown. The COVID-19 pandemic reimagined instruction for students of all ages and stages of learning. Although online schooling had been in place for decades, it became the only option for everyone, and it brought along uncertainty, isolation, death, and—for some—mental instability. Overnight, higher education as well as traditional K–12 systems of schooling were affected by this global pandemic; inequities were exacerbated (Griffith 2020), such as health disparities and the opportunity to work from home (McKee and Delgado 2020). Rashida was in that small percentage of the workforce that could work from home. A video-conferencing platform called Zoom was her primary mode of communication. As a result, Rashida's final classes were remote, and her time to conduct research increased.

The abrupt spread of COVID-19 also changed the dynamic of the cohort's interactions. As educators, most cohort members were fatigued with daily Zoom meetings, and by the time weekend classes were in session, everyone was exhausted. Conducting research under normal circumstances was difficult when juggling a full-time job, being a parent, and being a wife. Rashida used to look forward to her weekends on campus because she could simply focus on being a student.

During the spring of 2020, Rashida's home had been transformed into an office for her, a middle school for her daughter, and a high school for her son. The members of her family claimed their respective spaces inside their home to conduct daily business. Rashida's kids took over the dining room and family room while she worked in either their guest room or her bedroom. However, Rashida's husband continued to work outside of the home. Subsequently, isolation slowly set in as her family adjusted to their new routines of logging on to a computer daily.

To stay sane, Rashida worked outdoors when the weather permitted. She and her daughter took daily walks in their neighborhood, and her son rode his skateboard or played basketball in front of their home. Rashida worked on her dissertation every day for *more* than one hour.

She read articles and researched her topic. She revised and submitted drafts to her dissertation chair for feedback. She worked!

When it was time to schedule interviews with study participants, Rashida initially thought that using Zoom was going to be a problem; however, the opposite was true. The educators had become accustomed to the platform, and the convenience was unparalleled. Although Zoom made coordinating interviews easier, it lacked the face-to-face advantage of observing body language. However, her study participants' familiarity with Zoom allowed Rashida to complete all interviews within five weeks.

By this time, Rashida's White ally was two steps ahead of her in the dissertation process. They encouraged each other to persist through text messages. Comparatively, one Black counterpart, Rashida's friend with whom she entered the program, was the only other person who kept in touch. Rashida felt alone at this stage.

Her dissertation chair became sick and announced that he would retire soon. Communication between chair and student lessened during the weeks before his death. "You are almost finished!" "You are so close!" "I am so proud of you!" These are the words of encouragement Rashida received from her chair before he passed away. Their last text exchange the week before he died had nothing to do with her dissertation. Rashida prayed for him and sent words of encouragement. He responded by thanking her for her faithful prayers. Rashida's chair died on Sunday, August 8, 2021. Rashida defended her dissertation on Wednesday, September 29, 2021. It was an emotional day.

LESSONS LEARNED

1. *Find community to support you during your journey:* Adumene (2018) posits that female students of color will persevere in a higher-education environment when an empowering space is available. Rashida built a safe, supportive community through family, her mentor, one Black cohort member, one White advisor, and one unexpected White ally. This was just enough to network, address social issues, and reflect on her progress toward a terminal degree.

2. *Stay true to yourself:* When Rashida initially joined the cohort in 2018, she had feelings of inadequacy because she was not an administrator like most of the group. These feelings were short-lived once she learned her worth, discovered her God-given talents, and realized that she did belong. Her desire was always to effect change at the district level and work across departments to do so. Rashida stayed true to her goals and aspirations by seeking opportunities to grow and broaden her network. She was the first of three in her cohort to be published, she completed all assignments before anyone else, and she contributed to every class discussion by offering alternative perspectives from her role as a public school central office employee. She graduated on time.

3. *Stay focused on your goals:* Why not you? Rashida's goal was to attain a terminal degree in her profession. She also wanted to work at the district level in her school system. In the fall of 2018, the program advisor told the cohort during the first weekend of classes that his students often earned a job promotion as a result of the internship requirement. He likened it to a "yearlong interview." When Rashida began her internship in the spring of 2019, she was determined to prove that she could work at the district level. In winter 2020, she received that promotion.

4. *Take time to relax:* One significant factor in achieving a terminal degree was being organized and balancing work, school, and home life. Obtaining a timeline for due dates and milestones was paramount. Schedule time for yourself to relax and enjoy life.

REFERENCES

Adumene, Kile. 2018. *Female Students of Color in Higher Education.* Merrimack College. https://scholarworks.merrimack.edu/soe_student_ce/9.

Corley, Jacquelyn. 2020. "Where Are the Women of Color in Academia?" *Forbes*, June 27, 2020. www.forbes.com/sites/jacquelyncorley/2020/06/27/where-are-the-women-of-color-in-academia/?sh=57b7a0216401.

Davis, Shametrice, Leslie Reese, and Cecelia S. Griswold. 2020. "My Narrative Is Not What You Think It Is: Experiences of African Americans in a Doctor of Education Program." *International Journal of Doctoral Studies* 15: 199–216. https://doi.org/10.28945/4534.

Griffith, David. 2020. "There's No Place Like School." *Educational Leader-ship* 77, no. 8: 90–91.

McKee, Kimberly D., and Denise A. Delgado. 2020. "Three Ways to Help Women of Color and Indigenous Women Graduate Students Thrive." *Inside Higher Ed*, May 1, 2020. www.insidehighered.com/print/advice/2020/05/01/three-ways-help-women-color-and-indigenous-women-graduate-students-thrive-opinion.

Merriam-Webster. n.d. "Underdog." Accessed January 12, 2022. www.merriam-webster.com/dictionary/underdog.

National Center for Education Statistics. 2020. "Doctor's Degrees Conferred by Postsecondary Institutions, by Race/Ethnicity and Sex of Student." *Digest of Education Statistics*. https://nces.ed.gov/programs/digest/d20/tables/dt20_324.20.asp.

Patterson-Stephens, Shawna, and Estee Hernández. 2018. "Hermandad: Sista' Scholar Bonds for Black and Chicana Women in Doctoral Study." *Equity & Excellence in Education* 51, no. 3–4: 396–415.

Prince George's County Public Schools. n.d. "Executive Leadership Team." Accessed January 12, 2022. www.pgcps.org/offices/ceo/executive-team.

Young, Kathryn, and Myron Anderson. 2021. "Hierarchical Microaggressive Intersectionalities: Small Stories of Women of Color in Higher Education." *Metropolitan Universities* 32, no. 1: 78–103. https://doi.org/10.18060/24210.

CHAPTER 3

Resilience
A Prideful Term of Perseverance and Descriptor of Unspoken Challenges Endured

Bianca Nixon, Diamond Melendez, and Comfort Boateng

There are unspoken expectations among women of color, especially when applying to and preparing for doctoral programs and interviewing for employment opportunities. To project and present well during an interview, they must use their most professional voice, tame their hair, and present themselves as agreeable and unaggressive. Once offered a position, they might feel they must prove their worth, justifying not only to others but also to themselves that they are fit for academia. Not only is resilience characterized as perseverance and strength, but it is also a key ingredient for women of color to be successful in the fields of pharmacy and pharmaceutical sciences.

African American and Latina researchers alike may find it uncomfortable discussing the challenges in academia. The thought of how and where they fit within the systems of advantage and structural disadvantage in the academy is daunting, yet it is important to think about the ways social inequality is reproduced in higher education. Equally as important is the need to shed light on the stress that women of color face daily while striving to earn terminal degrees and ascend to their dream careers within academia.

Unfortunately, for many women of color or Black Indigenous People of Color (BIPOC) educators and researchers, the stress continues, almost feeling unsurmountable. Desperately needed is a safe space for women of color—particularly those working and researching in predominately White-male-dominated careers—to have an opportunity to tell their stories of the demanding responsibilities that accompany their ascension into the ranks of the professoriate. This chapter is such a space—the safe haven for three authors, all women of color, who proudly share their narratives.

This chapter focuses on the personal and professional journeys of three women of color to higher education at a private, predominately White institution. Included in their narratives are the challenges, successes, and points of intersectionality for each author's journey. The chapter opens with an explanation of social capital and intersectionality conceptual frameworks, as an explanation of how the authors' experiences intersect as they ascended to higher education, followed by a brief introduction of the chapter's three authors. The chapter concludes by offering four pearls of wisdom for aspiring women of color who dream of careers in pharmacy and/or the pharmaceutical sciences.

CONCEPTUAL FRAMEWORK

To understand the underrepresentation of women of color in STEM education—particularly in pharmacy and pharmaceutical sciences professions, the authors have used the concepts of social capital and intersectionality as undergirding frameworks for their narratives. These frameworks together will help illuminate forces that have potential for integrating and promoting women in pharmacy education and those that serve as barriers to career development and advancement.

Social Capital Perspectives

The concept of social capital has been widely viewed as a determinant of an individual's economic growth and a contributor to well-being of communities and nations, and has thus captured the attention of policymakers, researchers, educators, and community development practitioners alike (Alfred 2009). Many have credited the initial works of Bourdieu for advancing the concepts of social capital.

Bourdieu (1986) posits social capital has to do with structural relations and subjective beliefs that are associated with inequalities of resources and power. He further argues that inequality is caused by the unequal access to and interaction of various kinds of capitals, namely symbolic, cultural, and social. Bourdieu became interested in the ways that members of the middle and upper classes were able to capitalize on material and human resources inherent in networks and social groups to advance their own interests.

His significant contribution, therefore, is the interconnection of social capital and social inequalities and the importance of social capital as a source of power to advance one's interest and leverage one's position, in this case, in education and the chosen pharmacy career. Specifically, Bourdieu touts that social capital is an importance of communities as avenues for relationship building, support, networking, and career advancement for individuals who are often marginalized in academic and workspaces.

According to Putnam (2000), social capital serves both a bonding and a bridging function. As a bonding function, it tends to reinforce community values, cultures, and group homogeneity. As a bridging function, Putnam suggests that social capital can provide links to networks and acquaintances that are external to one's immediate community. As a career-development strategy, building communities within academic and work spaces provides opportunities for ethnic minorities to interact with community members who can provide the bridging capital not available in their immediate ethnic communities. For example, it is not unusual for Black and Hispanic women to have strong bonding relations with members of their cultural and religious groups, but they often have weak bridging ties that link them beyond their ethnocultural communities where the networking essential for career advancement and social mobility exists.

Intersectional Perspective

While the social capital perspective helps explain the structures that can support and advance women's academic and career pursuits, the intersectional perspective provides a more critical lens to explore the lack of representation among those who occupy spaces within the margins of what is considered mainstream culture. As Collins and Bilge (2016) explain, intersectionality as an analytic tool is useful to help uncover, explain, and illuminate the complexity of discrimination faced by people within spaces that were built to perpetuate a dominant power narrative of White, male, heterosexual, Christian norms. Yet these norms are "myths" in that they are socially constructed by people and continued by people who knowingly or unknowingly benefit from existing systems of power (Lorde 1980). STEM fields in both academia and business and industry, historically, are grounded in the values of the White majority that perpetuate these mythic norms.

Intersectionality explores sexism, patriarchy, racism, classism, and belief-ism. These "isms" impact the degree to which individuals are privileged or oppressed in societies and the conditions under which careers are developed and sustained. Furthermore, Cantor et al. (2014) assert, "The intersectional lens pushes us to ask new questions about the conditions under which talent can thrive" (p. 30), and remind us that to understand the absence and experiences of underrepresented groups and individuals in STEM, one needs to examine the issues with nuanced perspectives that cannot be captured through the broad dimensions of race or gender. Hence, the authors examined how three women's identities intersect to inform their experiences in academia and the workplace.

BEGINNING THEIR JOURNEYS

Camila Hernandez

Camila Hernandez began her journey to higher education in 2009 when she attended a four-year Historically Black College and received a bachelor of science degree in chemistry. From a family of educators, Camila loved science and always wanted to be a high school chemistry teacher. She also had a strong desire to help others. Soon Camila discovered that she could do both—teach and become a pharmacist.

Following her passions led Camila to professional school for four additional years to obtain a doctoral degree in Pharmacy (PharmD). Postgraduate training for Camila consisted of relocating to the Deep South to complete a twelve-month postgraduate residency in community-based pharmacy. Camila was the first African American resident to be accepted into this program. She then went on to complete a twelve-month postgraduate residency in ambulatory care pharmacy.

Upon completing her residency, Camila experienced a sense of accomplishment from multiple perspectives: first, taking the appropriate steps toward achieving her dream of being a teacher and pharmacist; and second, being a first-generation doctoral candidate. Having come from a supportive family who valued education, they provided a lot of internal familial success and congratulations. Little did Camila know this internal feeling of "Yes, I finally made it!" would be short-lived.

Skye Martinez

Skye Martinez always knew she wanted to be a pharmacist. In middle school she helped her grandmother manage her medications. "Blazing a path into a career in higher education as a young, Latina and Black woman was hard." And Skye, a first-generation college student, felt that there was very little guidance or support on how to navigate as an undergraduate student in a predominately White institution (PWI). There were very few students who shared Skye's background or cultural perspectives. Like many other women of color in similar positions, she had to quickly adapt to college life and learn new things (e.g., how to submit a financial aid application and course registration). Despite her lack of knowledge and exposure to college culture, Skye persevered and graduated with honors with a bachelor of science degree in biology from a prestigious four-year college.

Soon afterward, she was admitted into a four-year graduate level pharmacy program at a top ten pharmacy school in the nation. After obtaining her doctor of pharmacy degree, Skye continued her education and clinical training as the first and only woman of color resident at a vigorous twelve-month postdoctoral program. Skye's clinical rotation helped solidify her desire to become a professor in a pharmacy program. Skye began her academic appointment at a private institution in a professional doctoral program. The many years she devoted to education and postdoctoral training paid off, as she obtained an amazing position in academia; however, for all the successes throughout the journey, there were just as many challenges.

Mavis Agyemang

Mavis Agyemang was born and raised in Africa, where she received a bachelor of science in chemistry. Mavis's love for science was nurtured in her community by her grandfather, who was a traditional medicinal herbalist and loved science and experimenting with natural products. In Africa, the limited number of Black women in science can be attributed to Black girls being discouraged from going to school and encouraged to stay at home to complete household chores. Fortunately, this was not the case for Mavis, as her parents were supportive of her obtaining an education.

Mavis's academic record earned her an opportunity to move to the United States, to attend a large Historically Black College/University (HBCU), and to pursue her doctor of philosophy (PhD) degree in pharmaceutical sciences, with a specialization in medicinal chemistry. It was at this HBCU where Mavis received enormous support from other women of color.

THEIR GRADUATE SCHOOL EXPERIENCES

Camila

Many first-generation doctoral students coming from HBCU undergraduate institutions experience culture shock upon entering a PWI. Many BIPOC or women of color experience so much trauma and adversity while obtaining a doctoral degree that imposter syndrome quietly starts to creep in during important moments that normally warrant celebrations. Tulshyan and Burey (2021) loosely define *imposter syndrome* as doubting your abilities and feeling like a fraud. This feeling disproportionately affects high-achieving people, who find it difficult to accept their accomplishments. Many women, especially women of color, question whether they are deserving of accolades.

To Camila, it almost appeared as if the work was never done. She felt that in the blink of an eye, she went from being an undergraduate student—in the majority and around others who shared cultural similarities and who understood her background—to becoming one of only four minority students, out of a class of 140 students. This was a sudden shift from being in the top 10 percent of the class to having to prove your worth daily to both professors and fellow students, which proved to be more daunting than expected.

An added layer of self-doubt set in as she questioned if she was good enough and whether she belonged there. More importantly, Camila began to wonder why her group contributions were not being recognized like those of her counterparts. In one incident, while taking a group test with students in her class, when Camila voiced and offered a rationale for her answer, she was met with great reluctance; however, when the same answer was restated by a non-minority student, the answer was readily accepted by the group. Camila had countless instances like this throughout her pharmacy school trajectory.

Skye

Skye's overall experience in graduate school was surprisingly pleasant. The university embodied diversity and inclusion, and she thrived in that environment. For the first time, she was surrounded by other women with similar interests and goals. Finally, Skye had others around her who could relate to the internal doubt and exhaustion accompanied by pleasant feelings of victory for making it so far into their careers. There was a diverse set of professors with unique life experiences and vast knowledge to share with students. Skye's peers were from all walks of life, and the integration of so many beautifully different students into one program was remarkable.

The social culture of the graduate program was supportive, unlike her previous program had been. And while there were still tough times and barriers to overcome during four years of graduate school, she felt acceptance, made connections with fellow classmates, and was thankful for finding the right fit for her graduate studies. Skye had found her place to grow personally and professionally in an environment that reassured her of her full potential.

Mavis

As an immigrant, it was initially difficult for Mavis to transition into U.S. culture. There were challenges as a woman with a foreign accent. People sometimes ignored or responded poorly to Mavis by acting as if they did not understand what she was saying. Despite these challenges, Mavis received the best training and mentorship at a large HBCU. As an immigrant, Mavis felt reassured in this new arena of education and decided to step out of her comfort zone and initiate discussions with professors and fellow students. The diversity within her advisor's laboratory group not only provided a culture of support and collegiality but also fostered a nurturing yet challenging research environment.

Mavis's principal investigator (PI), a male of color, was one of the most outstanding mentors she had ever worked with. He was meticulous in his deliberations, held high expectations for all graduate students, and worked hard to encourage graduate students to develop their own areas of research. As reflected in Mavis's experiences at this HBCU, most of the professors were striving for the best for their students, and they were outstanding mentors. The mentorship received from others in the BIPOC community led Mavis to publish research findings in peer-reviewed journals, attend national conferences, and advance as a scientist. The astonishing training from this HBCU provided the foundation for Mavis's career as a quality professor.

POSTDOCTORAL EXPERIENCES

Camila Hernandez, PharmD

The postgraduate residency cycle is the most competitive atmosphere within a graduate student's life. And many minorities, particularly females, find themselves working twice as hard to be interviewed by programs. Upon being granted an interview, the "About Me" presentation topic stumps many women of color, including Camila. Deciding which hairstyle is most "professional," along with determining how much "personality" is revealed during the interview is always a delicate balancing act. Contrary to popular belief, women of color do not always know how they will be perceived during a one-on-one or group interview. Sadly, everyone's experience does not always have a happy ending.

Camila, being the first Black resident in a program that focused on serving the underserved, allowed the impact on patient care to be twice as beneficial coming from a BIPOC in comparison to those who served as residents in previous years. During many patient visits at the diabetes management clinic, patients would state, "I appreciate seeing someone who looks like me," or "I am so proud of you for becoming a pharmacist."

Internally, the relief she felt when discovering that some residents in neighboring residency programs were also minority students brought instant gratification. Even before introductions, Camila noted that the color of their skin alone radiated happiness into the atmosphere. There is an unspoken "connection" between like-minded individuals that can be sensed within the first five minutes of an encounter. BIPOC tend to gravitate toward one another in these instances and help guide one another to the common end goal, in this case—the successful completion of residency.

Skye Martinez, PharmD

There is something unsettling about being a young minority woman trying hard to advance in a career while simultaneously understanding and fitting into the organization's culture and continuously feeling the need to prove your worth. For Skye, being the first and the only one was exhausting. Skye experienced many firsts early within her career. For instance, she was the first minority woman in a highly regarded postgraduate program, the first in an accomplished position held previously by only White individuals, and the only BIPOC woman serving on coveted committees or boards.

Needless to say, no one in many of the academic and pharmacy spaces that Skye traveled looked like her. Skye had abundantly curly and volumized hair accompanied by bronzed skin, and a full-body figure. For many women of color, being the first, coupled with the pressures associated with maintaining the persona of effortlessly being superwoman, resulted in Skye being psychologically drained from racial battle fatigue. Nevertheless, throughout the journey to become a BIPOC woman in higher education, Skye became accustomed to being psychologically exhausted and to the dismissiveness and insensitivity from non-BIPOC peers as she excelled in her research and teaching.

Often, Skye's superiors were White men who simply could not relate and generally did not try, and colleagues were similar. Lack of diversity in the work environment can be harmful. From Skye's perspective, as a BIPOC woman who completed a postdoctoral program with only White counterparts, the lack of diversity perpetuated feelings of disconnect and often served as the impetus of racial battle fatigue. Smith (2004) indicated that racial battle fatigue is likely to occur when a person of color reacts to the disturbing conditions in dealing with racism in their everyday work life.

Racial battle fatigue is also the physical, mental, and emotional manifestation of racial microaggressions. Microaggressions are subtle, unconscious, layered, and increasingly spoken and unspoken insults directed at people of color based on race and other distinguishing characteristics that cause unnecessary stress on Blacks while benefiting Whites (Smith, Yosso, and Solórzano 2006). Over time, these racial microaggressions can cause various forms of mental, emotional, and physical stress. For African Americans and other people of color, the continuous exposure to and accrual of racial microaggressions can cause severe racial battle fatigue. Working somewhere that does not actively address or foster a caring and inclusive environment is tough. However, BIPOC women are tougher. BIPOC women must rise above it all, remain resilient and strong, and prove that they can and will succeed.

Mavis Agyemang, PhD

Mavis joined the federal research lab for her postdoctoral training. She can recall her first few days at the federal research laboratory. Mavis was surprised and felt lonely because of how few underrepresented minorities were present within her federal research institution. She also realized that most of the postgraduate fellows were coming from Ivy League schools and sometimes looked down on fellows from HBCU schools and frequently discounted their experiences. Other fellows had varied experiences or more extensive exposure to complex scientific methods, in which Mavis was lacking. She did not let this hinder her productivity, because she believed that Black women can rise above, and she would prove that she was even smarter than most of her peers.

Thankfully, Mavis met another African American woman, and they instantly bonded and became each other's keeper. She was also blessed to receive the best training and mentorship from her postdoctoral PI, who happened to be a White woman. Her laboratory was very diverse, with postdoctoral fellows from all different countries. Mavis's PI really knew how to communicate with immigrants, especially Black women, and this was appreciated. This PI is one of the most outstanding mentors Mavis had ever worked with. She closely monitored Mavis's postgraduate scientific research, and she never failed to demonstrate constant dedication to her work. Her postdoctoral training at the federal research laboratory under this supportive mentorship provided the foundation for Mavis's current work in neuroscience.

FROM POSTDOCTORAL STUDENT TO JUNIOR FACULTY

Camila Hernandez, PharmD, Assistant Professor of Clinical Sciences

Camila's decision to pursue higher education was rooted in a strong desire to not only educate others but also be a role model to those Black and Brown students who constantly find themselves being granted acceptance into a class to meet a "diversity quota," yet lacking a sense of community and mentorship once they are admitted. Students from various backgrounds all share a common theme of wanting to become pharmacists; however, they don't all receive the same support to aid in their success. As a minority woman in higher education, Camila and others had to navigate a sense of belonging with the complexity of outer appearance, hair, appropriate terminology, and being present as their own identities.

It should be noted that for many women of color in higher education, their personal identities are frequently connected to the identities of minority students in the respective academic programs. Moreover, when BIPOC women are asked, "How do you foresee being involved in helping us recruit students from local HBCUs?" or "What can we do to support our minority students once they arrive?" many women deem these questions as indicators of an expectation for them to shoulder the responsibilities for all minority students. It's almost as if there is an assumption that all BIPOC persons have all the answers to all minority-student-focused questions—yet again adding to the growing list of pressures minority women in higher education already face. Camila quickly came to the realization that she would serve as the "face of diversity, equity, and inclusion" for her institution.

Camila's hope is that as more and more BIPOC women share their stories, they will be read by those White counterparts to educate and help shed light on the reality of BIPOC women. Each day will be a challenge, and each new endeavor will be a transition; however, with resilience and the right attitude, Camila knows she will continue to break barriers and succeed in all that she does. The positive outcome from these experiences is a constant reminder that Camila can continue to create a path for other women of color to follow even despite the hurdles she has had to face.

Skye Martinez, PharmD, Assistant Professor of Clinical Sciences

Women of color who have finally made it into higher education still face many of the same challenges they faced when ascending to their positions. There are still colleagues and superiors who do not understand them and do not view their expertise or professional credentialing as an asset to the institution. These same colleagues are quick to label minority women as aggressive, disagreeable, or angry when they are simply exuding enthusiasm about their work or research. Behaviors such as these only exacerbate feelings of imposter syndrome and isolation from others who are vastly different from you. Little do they know that just below the surface of a woman of color's confidence level resides self-doubt.

To combat feeling out of place in academia, women of color—and specifically Skye, in this instance—prescribe to the "strong Black woman schema" (Harris-Lacewell 2001). The strong Black woman schema is an amalgamation of beliefs and cultural expectations of incessant resilience, independence, and strength that guide meaning-making, cognition, and behavior related to Black womanhood. As a result of continuously conjuring resilience as a response to physical and psychological hardships, many Black women have mastered the art of portraying strength while concealing trauma—a balancing act often held in high esteem among Black women.

A career in higher education is not much different than the path traveled to reach this destination. After obtaining an assistant professor position, Skye continued to feel the need to prove her worth, justifying not only to others but also to herself that she is fit for academia.

Nevertheless, she knew after years of education and training that one should feel validated in their experiences and knowledge. Finally, Skye was in a position where she had numerous degrees, licenses, certifications, and titles and could afford to be at ease because her accomplishments spoke volumes about the education and credentials so righteously received.

There are faculty at her institution and other programs who look like her, and BIPOC graduate students who look up to her. Skye knew she was in a place where she could help make a difference in others' lives and felt the most empowered she had in her career thus far. She now had the tools to actively engage in healthy coping methods for racial fatigue that have accumulated over the years, and an established support system in her personal and professional life. Tackling so many challenges to become a BIPOC woman in higher education created so many success stories. Skye believed that these challenges and successes should be shared with others for affirmation and motivation, and as a testimony of resilience.

Mavis Agyemang, PhD, Assistant Professor of Basic Pharmaceutical Sciences

Mavis transitioned from a fellow in postdoctoral training to a faculty position and independent research in higher education at a private PWI. When she initially joined her new faculty team, she was not only the sole African in the graduate program but also the only woman in her department. In terms of diversity, the environment was vastly different from her experiences in graduate school and during postdoctoral training. Mavis felt very lonely with no one who looked like her around. There was a lack of mentorship and a lack of diversity, which felt overwhelming.

Initially, she felt uncomfortable communicating with other colleagues. To overcome this, Mavis again stepped out of her comfort zone and worked with them together on projects and on committee assignments. Despite her efforts, overall, there was a lack of research mentorship, difficulties securing funding to support her research, and a lack of diversity, to include women of color—all of which made Mavis's transition to her new faculty position even more difficult.

Despite these difficulties, Mavis not only has found her research niche but also has found her voice as a tenure-track assistant professor. This, coupled with receiving a major extramural federal grant, was one of the many milestones and accomplishments in Mavis's career. Mavis currently serves as a strong female role model of underrepresented minority research scientists.

THEIR PEARLS OF WISDOM

Women of color in higher education exemplify hard work and dedication. They are determined, goal-oriented, and illustrious. Nevertheless, as described throughout this chapter, the journey into this professional career can be taxing. How is it that three women whose paths never crossed have so many commonalities in their professional careers? This attests to the fact that although the paths of women of color may not intersect, the challenges and experiences—both spoken and unspoken—are common.

However, for the authors of this chapter, no matter how challenging the journey, they continued to strive for success and accomplished their goals. And to date, they continue to do so each day upon arriving on campus, working in settings that lack diversity in classrooms and leadership. Against this backdrop, they collectively offer the following four pearls of wisdom to aspirant women of color who seek careers in education, pharmacy, or pharmaceutical sciences.

1. *Find the right institutional fit.* The climate of a university is a telling indication of how long you might stay. This is especially important as you choose a graduate program. Consider your fit for the institution and the intended department. Women of color are not provided with research and teaching opportunities in the same numbers as their White counterparts. During faculty job interviews, ask about the campus climate in relation to race. Inquire about the number of minority faculty on campus, and ask whether their research is supported.
2. *A good support system is priceless.* Garnering support from faculty and finding quality mentoring are instrumental for a

successful career in academia. This is especially important for women of color. The lack of support and substantive mentorship can lead to feelings of rejection for women of color, who are likely to be isolated in the pharmaceutical space.

3. *Be proud of the unique perspective you bring.* As with all professional pursuits, it is important to find your voice and be confident in the unique perspective you lend to a discussion. Women of color existing in predominately White male spaces have the opportunity to disrupt stereotypes and biases because the lenses they bring to the discourse probably had not been previously seen or heard. Always believe in yourself, and always bet on you. Have confidence in your brown skin.

4. *Paying it forward is important.* With great power comes great responsibility. Once a woman of color enters higher education, they owe it to the profession to willingly help mentor and support BIPOC students, graduates, and new faculty. Create opportunities for others to feel comfortable and thrive by cultivating an inclusive and safe environment. Contribute to research surrounding diversity, equity, inclusion, and antiracism when possible. Become an innovator and an ally for other BIPOC women who are interested in higher education. Guidance and support are needed so BIPOC women advancing in academia can face a little less adversity, demonstrate resilience only when needed, and flourish with unbounded success.

REFERENCES

Alfred, M. V. 2009. "Social Capital Theory: Implications for Women's Networking and Learning." *New Directions for Adult & Continuing Education* 122: 3–12.

Bourdieu, P. 1986. "The Forms of Capital." In *The Handbook of Theory and Research for Sociology of Education*, edited by J. G. Richardson, 645–68. New York: Greenwood.

Cantor, N., K. M. Mack, P. McDermott, and O. L. Taylor. 2014. "If Not Now, When? The Promise of STEM Intersectionality in the Twenty-First Century." *Peer Review* 16: 29–31.

Collins, P. H., and S. Bilge. 2016. *Intersectionality*. Cambridge, UK: John Wiley.

Harris-Lacewell, M. 2001. "No Place to Rest: African American Political Attitudes and the Myth of Black Women's Strength." *Women and Politics* 23: 1–34.

Lorde, A. 1980. "Age, Race, Class, and Sex: Women Redefining Difference." *In Women in Culture: An Intersectional Anthology for Gender and Women's Studies*, 16–22. Chichester, UK: John Wiley & Sons.

Putnam, R. D. 2000. *Bowling Alone: The Collapse and Revival of American Community*. New York: Simon & Schuster.

Smith, W. A. 2004. "Black Faculty Coping with Racial Battle Fatigue: The Campus Racial Climate in a Post–Civil Rights Era." In *A Long Way to Go: Conversations about Race by African American Faculty and Graduate Students*, edited by D. Cleveland, 171–90. New York: Peter Lang.

Smith, W. A., T. J. Yosso, and D. G. Solórzano. 2006. "Challenging Racial Battle Fatigue on Historically White Campuses: A Critical Race Examination of Race-Related Stress." In *Faculty of Color: Teaching in Predominantly White Colleges and Universities*, edited by C. A. Stanley, 299–327. Bolton, MA: Anker.

Tulshyan, R., and J. Burey. 2021, February 11. "Stop Telling Women They Have Imposter Syndrome." *Harvard Business Review*. https://hbr.org/2021/02/stop-telling-women-they-have-imposter-syndrome.

CHAPTER 4

"Voluntold"
A Framework for Contextualizing Black Women's Negative Experiences in the Academy
Marie Parfait-Davis

The negative experiences of Black women professionals in higher education can be attributed to a myriad of reasons. These barriers include being clustered in specific disciplines, navigating racist microaggressions, recruitment, and a slow process to tenure or retainment. Another often-unaddressed contributor that leads to unsavory conditions is the exhaustion Black women exhibit when "voluntold" to be responsible for analyzing and explaining social injustices to their colleagues. Despite these challenges, Black women continue to show up and break generational curses, shatter glass ceilings, and shift paradigms in various departments within the academy. It is time for Black women to take control of the "voluntold" narrative. Reimagining a future where Black women control what stories they tell, why and when they are told, and to whom is a critical first step to interrupting structural inequity, shaping our next generation of leaders, breaking trauma bonds, and creating a path to wellness.

The morning of Wednesday, September 23, 2020, I took part in a scheduled Zoom meeting with colleagues to discuss how we would navigate moving forward virtually with the students, parents, and community members we serve. The meeting agenda outlined that we would discuss logistics, registration links, virtual class formats, and resources that would be provided for families. It also outlined how we would continue to be accountable for our work and deadlines. In retrospect, it was a meeting much like many others that I took part in at the height of the pandemic, when companies, school systems, and organizations were learning how to transition into uncharted territory. It was also the morning the grand jury decided not to indict two of the three officers involved in the death of twenty-six-year-old EMT worker Breonna Taylor.

In my lifetime, I had witnessed many injustices toward Black men, women, and children at the hands of police officers, community vigilantes, or business owners. It immediately brought up memories of Sean Bell, Amadou Diallo, Yusef Hawkins, Latasha Harlins, and Trayvon Martin. Some of these stories I can't revisit or watch documentaries on because the pain is still real, still raw, even after all these years. The list is exhausting. However, somehow hearing that essentially no one would be held accountable for the death of Breonna Taylor hit me a little differently. I cannot say I was surprised. In fact, history has shown me time and time again that I should not have been.

Perhaps the myriad of emotions I felt that morning was a collective cry for all of those who have been unjustly killed and whose name many of us fail to remember. In any event, I could not show up as my authentic self during that meeting, particularly when the country was embroiled in several acts of social unrest across the nation. There was no acknowledgment, no pause, no asking if anyone was okay. This may have gone unnoticed, or even accepted, if not for the fact that our organization had recently taken steps to incorporate self-care check-ins, and an equitable approach to meeting agendas, discussions, and hiring, to establish a more inclusive, race conscious, and responsive workplace environment.

After months of diversity training, and the importance of cultural relevancy to our specific roles and responsibilities, I found it necessary and in alignment to our new learning and practices to willingly volunteer to stop the meeting and discuss with my colleagues how I was mentally and emotionally entering the meeting that day. Using a well-known research-based protocol that we had all adopted for workspace committee-meeting norms, I shared important wonderings of how racial inequities, and the most recent incident specifically, may have an impact on our student body and community.

At the end of the meeting, my committee chair and I discussed other ways we could continue to incorporate the protocol on race conversations into future committee and faculty meetings, advising sessions, and research team collaborative work. Together we outlined a strategic plan on how to incorporate healthy racial dialogue and provide engaging ways we can center ourselves and our colleagues in equity and inclusion, and how to confront our own biases and privilege to improve student outcomes and sense of security.

Upon reflecting on our meeting, I realized that I volunteered to provide insight and conversation on social inequities on my terms. I used our organizations' foundational work on race conversations as a tool to discuss the impact of recent events on my work specifically, but also suggested the implications the events may have on the collective student body, and how they would react, as well as our relationship with outside partnerships/stakeholders.

In contrast, a "voluntold" experience may have appeared strikingly different. *Voluntold* or *Voluntell* is a fairly new term used to describe being forcefully assigned a task (usually unpleasant or uncomfortable in nature) by a boss or supervisor (Collins Dictionary 2012). In times of social unrest, similar to what was occurring in society during my Zoom meeting, or to satisfy a company's equity mandates, many Black women are "voluntold" to unpack centuries of systemic harm, violence, racist behavior, and prejudicial mindsets for organizations. They are asked to do this all while still grappling with those very same attitudes and very real repercussions themselves. Many stay silent, while others unwillingly trudge forward because of their inability to say no, to save face, their reputation, or even their job.

In *Their Eyes Were Watching God*, Zora Neale Hurston writes, "If you are silent about your pain, they'll kill you and say you enjoyed it." I hope we no longer remain silent; I hope we choose us first; I hope we take up space, find the courage to say no, and take care of ourselves.

THE CONCEPT OF "VOLUNTOLD"

The word *voluntold* is the combination of the words *volunteer* and *told*. To volunteer for something is to participate partially or fully in a task of one's free will. The word *voluntold*, however, takes this idea and essentially turns it on its head. The term gives the illusion of choice, while simultaneously leaving recipients of the word feeling pressured to complete a task. The pressure may derive from fear of being "black-listed," isolated, taken off important projects, derailing an upward trajectory at work, or being seen as not a team player.

The word may have its origins in the military, specifically the Marines, dating as far back as the early 1970s ("Voluntold" 2008). In this environment, commanding officers may have suggested they would like volunteers to complete a task; however, they did not wait for petty officers to volunteer, but they specifically named those officers who would fulfill the duty with little to no pushback. The word gained popularity in the early 1990s when it was first seen in pop culture. It truly became part of the American work and sports culture in the early 2000s ("Voluntold" n.d.).

Fast forward to today's higher-education spaces. Black women, although not officers in the military, are far too often "voluntold" to provide truths in times of peril for coworkers and colleagues in conferences, meetings, advising sessions, conference presentations, and lecture halls. Often, the truth is asked to be consumed so that it does not overwhelm the palate but can be taken in small bites. In these spaces, Black women are directed, and prompted, to be the resident expert on all subjects that seem cultural, diverse, or ethnic. Some may feel obligated to comply in an effort to avoid becoming bitter and burdened by the task. It can leave one feeling exhausted trying to help so-called allies engage in performative activism.

Black women traditionally fall under a myriad of interconnected social categorizations that help keep us marginalized and our voices silenced or undervalued. Often, Black women fight to have our voices heard, and in doing so, some may feel privileged to have been chosen to speak for or represent the vast majority of their race during social unrest, equity training, or diversity hiring fairs. This may be because, again, being "voluntold" gives the illusion of choice. However, it is critical to note that being "voluntold" to address systemic oppression all while having no input in the creation of sustainable policy changes that dismantle systemic racism is akin to White people weaponizing Black voices to confirm deeply held biases and beliefs. Black women must interrupt the "voluntold" culture in order to disrupt negative experiences in higher education.

WHY WE CAN'T SAY NO: "VOLUNTOLD" AND BLACK WOMEN'S HISTORY—A TRAUMA BOND

When examining the effects of being "voluntold" in the BIPOC community, it is imperative that we examine how our responses may be rooted in generational trauma. Populations that are systematically exploited and endure continued abuse, racism, and poverty are more at risk of experiencing generational trauma (Gillespie 2020).

Historically, Black women have often been stripped of their ability to exercise freedom of choice and voice, or to exert power over their own agencies. This can be seen as far back as the forced, painful, and often-inhumane experiments on Black women's bodies by Dr. Marian Sims to advance the field of gynecology (Holland 2018) to the harvesting and reproducing of Henrietta Lacks's cells to advance medical research (Skloot 2010). Medical violence against Black women shows that this group is three times more likely to die during child delivery and that Black women's level of pain and discomfort are not taken seriously and are often dismissed (Centers for Disease Control and Prevention 2021; Daley 2020; Campbell 2021). In each of these examples, Black women may have been given the illusion of choice, were misinformed before providing consent, were not given any alternative options, or were led to believe that physical harm may come if they said no.

This lack of choice throughout generations often led to a glaring unspoken truth: when Black women are "voluntold" at work, as a patient in a hospital, as a member of a search committee, or in other spaces of higher education, they may not think saying no is a viable option. Culturally, Black girls and Black women may have been conditioned—either consciously or unconsciously—to stay silent. Generational trauma can be nuanced and inadvertently implied throughout someone's life and extends from one generation to the next (Gillespie 2020; Green 2017). Consequently, over time, Black women are less likely to protest or resist requests of their time and intellectual property as they get older. Saying no has proven to be detrimental to both the physical and mental health of Black women (Evans, Bell, and Burton 2017; West 2003).

An act of resistance can lead to physical harm and even death at higher rates for Black women. Evidence of this is apparent in the countless cases of Black women being killed or seriously injured as a result of dismissing advances of men who felt entitled to a Black woman's time or body (Evans, Bell, and Burton 2017; West 2003). Black women are twice as likely to be murdered by men than White women, and 92 percent of these killings are intra-racial. Subsequently, domestic violence is the number-one health issue facing Black women (Blackburn Center 2020).

We must ask ourselves how this historical generational trauma and fear of repercussions of saying no translates into the workspaces and job duties of Black women in higher education today, if at all. A reality that may need further investigation is that there may be a correlation between Black women being singled out as the resident expert—and essentially forced without compensation to lead conversations—and their chronicled collective inability to say no or decline these requests because of anticipated backlash and generational trauma.

Who most often holds positions of power in the workplace, and how do Black women perceive that power? In Fortune 500 companies, 85 percent of senior executives are White males, and they often set the tone of the workplace (Roberts and Mayo 2019). When a Black woman is "voluntold" to complete a committee assignment, for example, she may experience acts of misogyny because of how Black women are portrayed in the media both historically and currently. Soave (2019) suggests that Black women live in the midst of two kinds of discrimination, racism, and sexism, and thus are uniquely discriminated against.

As Jennifer Farmer describes, "Black women in the workforce always have two jobs—what they are employed to do and surviving all of the extra tasks that come with false stereotypes" (quoted in Watkins 2021). For example, the objectification of Black women perpetuates the notion that our physical attributes are our greatest quality. We see this portrayed countless times in the way the media hypersexualizes Black women's bodies (Matthews 2018). The excessive sexualization of Black women causes harm to both the observer and the victim. It reinforces the notion that Black women's voices are not as important or valued as their bodies. As a result, when Black women do speak up or use their voices, they are overwhelmingly seen as disruptive, loud, and combative. Therefore, while working on that committee assignment, a Black woman may painstakingly be committed to combatting the association of the quality of her work to her physical shape, hair, and perceived aggressive attitude.

The emotional tax associated with being a Black woman in the American workplace is multifaceted and layered (Roberts and Mayo 2019). In an attempt to avoid being labeled as angry Black women or to prove their worth as intellectual and capable employees, many Black women unwillingly accept the role of a resident expert in order to dismantle or counteract these long-held misogynistic, patriarchal, and racist views. Many do so even if the area in which they are asked to lend analysis or solutions is not their area of expertise.

When not being objectified, Black women and their voices are invisible. The world of higher education can often fail to consider the lives of Black women and the conditions under which they navigate life, their labor, and how they engage at work (Jordan-Zachery and Floyd-Alexander 2018). Black women remain generally invisible to the male gaze outside of serving in predetermined and preconceived typecast roles. Those in positions of power are typically unresponsive to Black women's positionality except when they are needed for their voting bloc dominance (Jordan-Zachery 2017).

I am not suggesting that Black women are threatened or physically harmed when "voluntold." I am implying, however, that the collective and historical trauma of being made to complete tasks against their will may lead to the perception that Black woman are unable to fully use their voices to say no. Additionally, violence against Black women and their bodies, as well as their perceived invisibility, may in fact play a role in examining why it may be difficult to reject being "voluntold."

RECOGNIZING AND FIGHTING AGAINST "VOLUNTOLD" CULTURE

Anti-Blackness and sexism still exist in many workspaces. These issues, along with microaggressions and micro-invalidations, pervade Black women's lives and reject their contribution and importance to the labor force (Daley 2020). These setbacks impede Black women in resisting a "voluntold" work culture. There is a particular way that Black women are subordinated and are only protected to the extent that their existence and opinions align with that of White women or men

(Crenshaw 1989). Hence, the response of being "voluntold" is akin to walking a tightrope, trying desperately to remain balanced, while avoiding very real threats to one's success at work. However, more and more Black women are calling out incidents of being "voluntold," and it correlates to their dehumanization.

The dehumanization of Black women is prevalent across all societal norms. While their voices are eliminated from social discourse, they are still used to magnify feminist platforms as mascots. Take Tarana Burke, for instance, the creator and founder of the #MeToo movement, but not the face of it at the onset. For a long time, that hashtag and subsequent work was attributed to White women, even though Tarana Burke began this campaign over ten years ago as an effort to aid under-privileged women of color affected by sexual abuse and share her own personal story of abuse (Woodson 2018). Instead, the movement is known more for the elite White women who have spoken out against assault within the entertainment industry. Many Black women have been instrumental in volunteering to tell the story of Tarana Burke and her work so as not to erase or misplace her legacy.

Recently many White feminists came out in droves on social media to criticize the title of the movie *King Richard* (Bailey 2021; Johnson 2021). The movie highlighted how a Black man helped his daughters, Venus and Serena Williams, become the most decorated tennis players in history. White women focused on the fact that the movie is about women but centers a man in its name. They called it benevolent sexism and said they were speaking up for Black women. This is despite the fact that both Venus and Serena Williams had full creative control of the movie and wanted to pay homage to their father (Bailey 2021; Johnson 2021). We see it culturally when cornrows are called boxer braids, or when Black girls are suspended because of wearing their natural hair to school (Battle 2017; Jacobs and Levin 2018). Black woman writers, social media influencers, and magazine reporters were instrumental in getting these stories out in the public in an effort to control the narrative.

When Black women's voices are not being erased, they are being used as symbols for protection, masculinity, and strength. Think of the cover of Colin Kaepernick's (2021) book *Abolition for the People: The Movement for a Future Without Policing and Prisons*. The cover art is an image of a dark-skinned woman leading the charge against police brutality. While many Black women are on the front lines of the fight against injustice, they should not be the symbol for it (Calixte 2021). It continues to push the narrative that Black women are saviors, that they are superhuman, and are willing to take on the brunt of society's ills.

In another example to control the narrative, droves of Black women signed and collected a petition with over ten thousand signatures to change the cover art. Although Colin Kaepernick never responded or had the image removed, it helped to spark debates in lecture halls and in meetings demonstrating that Black women have the power to shift the culture on what is discussed and why when it comes to inequity.

We saw the same thing play out on the cover of *Rolling Stone* magazine during the height of civil unrest in the summer of 2020. A dark-skinned Black woman is depicted as the protector of an entire race. In the image, she is depicted as leading the charge for social justice while holding the hand of a Black male child, with no Black adult male figure in close proximity (Calixte 2021). Black women again protested the image and offered alternative solutions. By assertively addressing the blatant example of inequity, Black women offered another lens through which to examine structural racism and sexist storytelling.

Black women do not need to be "voluntold" to lead campaigns or discussions in areas where we are most often misunderstood and mis-represented. Let Black women decide which stories they want to tell and create the conditions in order for them to do so safely. Chimamanda Ngozi Adichie (2009) asserts that "the single story creates stereotypes, and the problem with stereotypes is not that they are untrue, but that they are incomplete. They make one story become the only story." The powers that be in higher academia should not be allowed to determine which stories Black woman lend their expertise to, if at all.

HOW WORKSPACES CAN FIGHT AGAINST A "VOLUNTOLD" CULTURE

After several months of political and social unrest, following the kill-ings of George Floyd, Breonna Taylor, Atiana Jefferson, and Botham Jean, many Black women found themselves being called on to provide clarity and context to colleagues within the work environment. In doing so, it is important that we begin to navigate and reject the superwoman stereotype (Evans, Bell, and Burton 2017). Black women should not be given the task to educate coworkers on the state of race and gender issues in America. Institutions must do the heavy lifting to dismantle and confront systemic racism and bias within their respective organizations. It cannot be the job of Black women to spearhead these efforts.

Volunteering one's time and expertise should never feel pressured. Ideally, giving one's time and thoughts to address societal ills should align with the company's overall vision and mission. There should be thoughtful ways on the part of the institution to make volunteering that addresses social injustice worthwhile and accessible to all, not just Black women. This can be done by engaging participants in ongoing trainings and professional development to establish norms and protocols about how to discuss race, racism, and inequity. This should be a part of the fabric of the organization.

Strategic leadership is needed that shifts the culture of how higher academia creates conditions to hold discussions regarding systemic and institutionalized racism across departments and teams. Workspaces can also adapt technology tools—such as mobile apps, surveys, and questionnaires—that help make everyone an active participant and contributor to the discussion of social injustice. Additionally, workspaces can ask participants to complete pre-work or tasks to give them a better understanding of the topic that will be discussed or tackled collectively. An established synergy should be the goal of volunteerism in order to promote creative cooperation between colleagues. This would bode well for Black women in the workplace and relieve them of consistently being identified as the obvious choice to discuss diversity and equity issues.

Companies and institutions should begin with the end in mind and be proactive in understanding the underlying dynamics of being "voluntold." Stephen Covey (1989) asserts that within our society, there is a highly integrated approach through which we develop effectively that includes dependence, independence, and interdependence. The goal is to become interdependent and have public victories of teamwork, cooperation, and communication. Companies and organizations should work on building a culture of trust, one where employees can be honest without fear of repercussions and backlash.

This is especially important for Black women, mainly because so few hold supervisory positions in the workplace. Black people account for only 8 percent of managers and 3.8 percent of CEOs in corporate America (Roberts and Mayo 2019). Furthermore, only 7 percent of U.S. higher-education administrators and 8 percent of nonprofit leaders are Black, yet Black workers are often tasked with leading conversations on cultural issues.

When companies ask their Black workers to lead such efforts without offering them safety and compensation or considering whether or not their employees feel like they can really say no, bosses risk replicating the same racist and unfair power structures they wish to eradicate within their organization (Walk-Morris 2020).

It is time that organizations reimagine how BIPOC women are "voluntold" to rationalize, explain, or justify how and why the system is broken. If we do not interrupt how things have always been done when it comes to our expectations of Black women in the workplace, then we run the risk of perpetuating the negative tropes that have existed for decades. Although the powers in control may be well-intentioned, it is their poor decision-making regarding "voluntold" directives that is long-lasting. These directives are often misaligned, ill-advised, and time-consuming and imply that Black women are not allowed to rest. Instead, they must continue to be on guard at all costs to help navigate spaces of comfortability for colleagues.

When leadership is disingenuous about the ways the collective voices of Black women are heard, they force Black women to participate in performative activism. This leads to a false sense of a positive climate and culture within the workspace. This illusion allows marginalization to thrive and ignores the effects of intersectionality that Black women face daily when being "voluntold." Therefore, rest for Black women is essential. Rest is resistance. As Audre Lorde (1988) so eloquently states, "Caring for myself is not self-indulgence, it is self-preservation, and that is an act of political warfare." Black women must rest in order to take care of themselves, take up space, and preserve their right to exist authentically and fully each day.

REFERENCES

Adichie, Chimamanda Ngozi. 2009, July. "The Danger of a Single Story." TED Talk, 18:33. www.ted.com/talks/chimamanda_ngozi_adichie_the_danger_of_a_single_story?language=en.

Bailey, Laquesha. 2021, November 27. "White Feminists Are Mad Venus and Serena Williams' Story Centres Their Dad." *Medium*. https://medium.com/fan-fare/white-feminists-are-mad-venus-and-serena-williams-story-centres-their-dad-3b10fbd209de.

Battle, Marquaysa. 2017, May 16. "8 Times Schools Let Black Girls' Hair Interfere with Their Education." *Elite Daily*. www.elitedaily.com/life/culture/black-girls-natural-hair-racism-schools/1953497.

Blackburn Center. 2020, February 26. "Black Women & Domestic Violence." www.blackburncenter.org/post/2020/02/26/black-women-domestic-violence.

Calixte, Christiane. 2021, June 12. "In Response to Colin Kaepernick's Book: The Dehumanization of Black Women." *The Blotter*. https://bcblotter.com/opinion/2021/06/12/in-response-to-colin-kaepernicks-book-the-dehumanization-of-black-women.

Campbell, Colleen. 2021. "Medical Violence, Obstetric Racism, and the Limits of Informed Consent for Black Women." *Michigan Journal of Race and Law* 26: 47–75.

Centers for Disease Control and Prevention. 2021. "Working Together to Reduce Black Maternal Mortality." Last modified April 9, 2021. www.cdc.gov/healthequity/features/maternal-mortality/index.html#:~:text=Supports%2025%20states%20through%20the,deaths%20and%20reduce%20racial%20disparities.

Collins Dictionary. 2012, November 12. "Voluntold." www.collinsdictionary.com/submission/7211/voluntold+.

Covey, Stephen. 1989. *The 7 Habits of Highly Effective People*. New York: Simon & Schuster.

Crenshaw, Kimberlie. 1989. "Demarginalizing the Intersection of Race and Sex: A Black Feminist Critique of Antidiscrimination Doctrine, Feminist Theory and Antiracist Politics." *University of Chicago Legal Forum*, article 8. https://chicagounbound.uchicago.edu/cgi/viewcontent.cgi?article=1052&context=uclf.

Daley, Patricia. 2020. "Lives Lived Differently: Geography and the Study of Black Women." *Royal Geographical Society* 52: 794–800.

Evans, Stephanie, Kanika Bell, and Nsenga Burton. 2017. *Black Women's Mental Health: Balancing Strength and Vulnerability*. Albany, NY: SUNY Press.

Gillespie, Claire. 2020, October 27. "What Is Generational Trauma? Here's How Experts Explain It." *Health*. www.health.com/condition/ptsd/generational-trauma.

Green, Susan. 2017, July 13. "Violence Against Black Women—Many Types, Far-Reaching Effects." Institute for Women's Policy Research. https://iwpr.org/iwpr-issues/race-ethnicity-gender-and-economy/violence-against-black-women-many-types-far-reaching-effects.

Holland, Brynn. 2018, December 4. "The 'Father of Modern Gynecology' Performed Shocking Experiments on Enslaved Women." History.com. www.history.com/news/the-father-of-modern-gynecology-performed-shocking-experiments-on-slaves.

Jacobs, Julia, and Dan Levin. 2018, August 21. "Black Girl Sent Home from School over Hair Extensions." *New York Times*. www.nytimes.com/2018/08/21/us/black-student-extensions-louisiana.html.

Johnson, Jeroslyn. 2021, November 23. "White Woman Sparks Debate after Accusing 'King Richard' Biopic of Being Sexist." *Black Enterprise*. www.blackenterprise.com/white-woman-sparks-debate-after-accusing-king-richard-biopic-of-being-sexist.

Jordan-Zachery, Julia. 2017. *Shadow Bodies: Black Women, Ideology, Representation and Politics*. New Brunswick, NJ: Rutgers University Press.

Jordan-Zachery, Julia, and Nikol Floyd-Alexander. 2018. *Black Women in Politics: Demanding Citizenship, Challenging Power and Seeking Justice*. Albany, NY: SUNY Press.

Kaepernick, Colin. 2021. *Abolition for the People: The Movement for a Future Without Policing and Prisons*. [United States]: Kaepernick Publishing.

Lorde, Audre. 1988. *A Burst of Light*. Ithaca, NY: Firebrand Books.

Matthews, Annalycia. 2018. "Hyper-Sexualization of Black Women in the Media." *Gender and Sexuality Studies, Student Work Collection* 22. https://digitalcommons.tacoma.uw.edu/gender_studies/22.

Roberts, Laura, and Anthony Mayo. 2019, November 14. "Toward a Racially Just Workplace." *Harvard Business Review*. https://hbr.org/2019/11/toward-a-racially-just-workplace.

Skloot, Rebecca. 2010. *The Immortal Life of Henrietta Lacks*. New York: Random House.

Soave, Robby. 2019, July. "Intersectionality 101." *Reason*. https://reason.com/2019/06/17/intersectionality-101.

"Voluntold." 2008, May 17. *A Way with Words* (podcast). www.waywordra-dio.org/voluntold.

"Voluntold." N.d. Dictionary.com. Accessed April 20, 2022. www.dictionary .com/e/slang/voluntold.

Walk-Morris, Tatiana. 2020, November 6. "Employers and Co-Workers Want Black Women's Expertise, but Are They Paying Them for It?" *The Guardian.* www.theguardian.com/us-news/2020/nov/06/employers-and-co -workers-want-black-womens-expertise-but-are-they-paying-them-for-it.

Watkins, D. 2021, March 24. "'Say "No" Nicely': Toxic Workplace Culture Demands Black Women Shrink Themselves and Never Speak Up." *Salon.* www.salon.com/2021/03/24/first-and-only-jennifer-farmer-black-women -workplace-racism-.

West, Carolyn. 2003. *Violence in the Lives of Black Women: Battered Black and Blue.* New York: Routledge.

Woodson, Robert. 2018, October 1. "How the Elite Hijacked the #METOO Movement." *The Hill.* https://thehill.com/opinion/civil-rights/408882-how -the-elite-hijacked-the-metoo-movement.

Part II

ADVANCING THROUGH

CHAPTER 5

The Work We Must Do
Toward an Understanding of How Early Career Black Women Faculty Navigate Their Place in Higher Education
Miyoshi Juergensen and Tamela C. Thomas

De [black] woman is de mule uh de world so fur as Ah can see.
—Zora Neale Hurston (in Bloom 2008, 14)

In Zora Neale Hurston's landscape-shifting text *Their Eyes Were Watching God*, the mule is frequently used to symbolize hard work, victimization, and subjugation. Indeed, the first mention is in reference to Black women, where Nanny, the protagonist's grandmother, explains their intergenerational reality: that the "[Black] woman is de mule uh de world." She then says, "Ah been prayin' fah it tuh be different wid you. Lawd, Lawd, Lawd!" (in Bloom 2008, 14). In accepting the disappointment of little progressive change and preparing her granddaughter for this reality, Nanny alerts the reader to a conscious understanding of the intersections between work, race, gender, and class at play in the novel; she also points to a springboard for exploring Black women's real-world work experiences in both historical and contemporary contexts.

This chapter is in that vein, as it is about Black women's work, specifically Black women's work as we begin our careers in the academy. It is about the work we are expected to do, the additional work we are asked to do, and the work we *must* do as early career Black women faculty interested in our communities' liberation, wholeness, humanity, and justice. For the purposes of this chapter, we focus on literary and theoretical frameworks designed by and for Black women to make sense of our personal experiences against the backdrop of our intersectional Blackness.

Ultimately, we draw from Zora Neale Hurston's (1937) mule symbolism, Alice Walker's ([1983] 2004) definition of *womanism*, Stephanie Shaw's (1996) research on Black professional women during Jim Crow, and Patricia Hill Collins's (2002) *Black Feminist Thought*. Finally, in our journey to become part of the 2.1 percent of Black females with tenure in the United States, we discuss implications for understanding with more precision the intersections of Black women's work in the academy, beginning with the early tenure-track years (June and O'Leary 2021).

OF WOMANIST, ENDARKENED, AND SISTERLY EPISTEMOLOGIES

Alice Walker ([1983] 2004) defines *womanism* as "a black feminist or feminist of color . . . committed to survival and wholeness of entire people" (370). Additionally, we operationalize *endarkened epistemologies* as ones we can "choose to be and think from . . . that declares that our lives [as Black women] matter . . . [as we] make sense of our lives against a Black backdrop" (Dillard 2016, 30). Given the foundation of both, we come to our work in the academy deeply connected to our Black womanhood as well as our collective histories, communities, and complex individual identities as women of color.

Following Dillard's (2016) theoretical framing of Black women's leadership in the workplace, we also invoke a spiritual component of our work with and for each other, the program, and the schooling communities served by our students. For example, what some might call coincidence, we call divine as we first met when we accepted our respective positions. That said, our ability to bring our womanist and endarkened epistemologies to our work is rooted in our shared values, norms, and sense-making regarding our commitment and proximity to Black women's intellectual excellence and ambition. Specifically, we are both HBCU graduates who share lifetime sorority membership to the same organization, were mentored by Black women academics who are giants in our field, and grew professionally in the fire of K–12 service to our schooling communities.

And so, we turn to womanism to underscore the sisterly solidarity between us in this work. We view ourselves as sisters in scholarship and service to each other, our communities, and ourselves. Additionally, as noted by Alice Walker's definition, a womanist is "not a separatist," and she has a long history of doing the hardest work in the name of all our liberation. Later in the definition, Walker writes that a Black woman is "traditionally capable, as in 'Mama, I'm walking to Canada and I'm taking you and a bunch of other slaves with me.' Reply: 'It wouldn't be the first time'" (Walker [1983] 2004, 370). Should our collaborative work in/for education matter in the ways we hope, we will not be the last to take a bunch of us toward freedom because we share similar training as scholars and as Black women.

MULE: THE METAPHOR THAT KEEPS ON GIVING

Nanny's astute observation of the similarities between the mule and the Black woman can be applied to the expectations experienced during our first year in higher education. From initial hire, the assignment from the university was clear: a high-enrollment graduate teacher leadership program was in shambles, and the new faculty would provide the vision and labor to (re)build a program lucrative in matriculation numbers commiserate with expectations for a university on the road to R2 Carnegie status. This would require a full curriculum overhaul for three different degree programs and one certification program, teaching the courses required for each degree, supporting the dissertation work of over sixty doctoral students, and staying current with (forget ahead of) personal research agendas and service to the university required for tenure and promotion.

While the idea of developing a comprehensive redesign of each program was overwhelming before the ink was dry on our contracts, that feeling of overwhelm was initially mitigated by the perceived opportunity to redesign an entire educational leadership program—and the only doctorate program in teacher leadership in the state—with two Black women at the helm who shared commitments to social justice; teacher autonomy; collaboration; and equity-centered educational policy, practice, and research.

Unfortunately, that first year in the academy was a blur of work-related fires that needed the attention of strong department and program

leadership. To support us as early career faculty, the program coordinator position was held by a tenured Black male colleague within
our department who had no experiences regarding teacher leadership.
At the outset, our colleague was transparent about his goals: to take
over the administrivia of program coordination so we could adjust to
our new positions. However, the reality of our college and program's
deficiencies required us to take on much of the unofficial coordinating
duties and culminated in our agreeing to co-coordinate the program by
the end of our first year as tenure-track faculty. Here, Nanny's mule
metaphor gives again:

> Maybe it's some place way off in de ocean where de black man is in
> power, but we don't know nothin' but what we see. So de white man
> throw down de load and tell de [Black] man tuh pick it up. He pick it up
> because he have to, but he don't tote it. He hand it to his womenfolks.
> (Hurston in Bloom 2008, 14)

Here is a solid example of good intentions leading to hellish work realities—or, as Nanny puts it, the man picking up the load because he has
to, but handing it to women instead of toting it.

Although our Black male colleague was well intentioned, his time
as coordinator seems to have been spent keeping the teacher leadership
program afloat by plugging holes as they exposed significant cracks.
Minor cracks (even those that spanned the lifetime of the program)
were ignored or shuttled to other people's inboxes, as he was upfront
about the temporary nature of his role and responsibilities. Thus,
when the opportunity to coordinate a smaller program elsewhere in
our department became available, our colleague took it, leaving our
department chair to ask us to carry the existing coordinating workload
by ourselves and execute the labor without clear or strategic structures
in place to support us with these newly assigned tasks.

WHAT BLACK WOMEN ACADEMICS OUGHT TO BE AND DO

Stephanie Shaw's (1996) *What a Woman Ought to Be and Do* examines
the social institutions that Black women were a part of during the Jim
Crow era and focuses on the processes and people that influenced how

Black women would define themselves and their work. In revisiting her book for this chapter, we first recognized the similarities between the women highlighted in the manuscript and the social responsibility we feel. Other similarities include the processes of socialization—social traditions, community support, and public pressure—that have been communicated to them and us, specifically in graduate school: that education is mission critical for the Black community.

For the purposes of the chapter, we use Shaw's work to outline the importance of the personal, social, and collective inputs guiding and supporting our trajectory in the academy. For us, the messages we received in graduate school, and continue to receive as current members of a departmental affinity group, signal that one of the practices Black women academics ought to embody is joining forces with like-minded Black women.

For us, we are fortunate to have the support of two recently tenured Black women faculty in our department. Given that Black women's experiences in the academy can be described as surviving in the margins (Souto-Manning and Ray 2007), our relationship with the other Black women in our department counters that narrative and provides the opportunity to center ourselves and our work in the programmatic practices associated with our department and institution. Importantly, like other affinity groups that serve Black women scholars (Allen and Joseph 2018), the type of support we receive helps us persist in higher education and gives us hope that our leadership, scholarship, and service will have an impact on other scholars in the margins.

Of note, Hurston's Nanny shows up in Shaw's work as well; in this context, however, Nanny tells us that she had to "take a broom and a cook-pot and throw up a highway through de wilderness" (Hurston in Bloom 2008, 29) for her daughter. In this example, the highway is a metaphor for the strategies Black people have used to pave the way for successive generations around the oppressive structures inherent to American society. The highway metaphor extends to our experiences preparing to enter the academy, as our graduate experiences employed pedagogies of intentionality (Croft et al. 2018) to throw up a highway for our successful completion of our doctorate degrees at Predominantly White Institutions.

Presently, in our own work in the academy, we throw up highways for currently practicing teachers, many of whom are either coming with or serving students who claim complicated and marginalized identity markers. That said, we believe that as Black women academics, we ought to see ourselves as both the beneficiaries and engineers of highways that bypass obstacles facing our communities.

BLACK FEMINIST THOUGHT AND INTERSECTIONALITY METHODOLOGY: FUTURE RESEARCH IMPLICATIONS

Black feminist thought (BFT) aims to describe the phenomenological experiences found at the intersection of sex and race for Black women and is carried out through the intense study of the relationships Black women have with self, community, history, and society (Hill Collins 2002; Allen and Joseph 2018). BFT encompasses both commonplace knowledge born of the everyday experiences of Black women and the expert knowledge derived from the analysis of the thoughts and theories of Black women scholars working for the advancement of Black women in broader society.

For the purposes of this chapter, we assert that Black women intellectuals bring a scholarly application of knowledge that is particular to Black women's intellectualism. As argued by Ladson-Billings (1995), our experiences outside of the ivory tower are legitimate, essential to informing BFT as pedagogy, and capable of critiquing the systems shaping the everyday lived experiences and practice of Black women in the academy.

A natural progression from BFT points us toward Haynes et al.'s (2020) intersectionality methodology (IM), which offers a rigorous and reflexive approach to researching how our early career experiences in the academy as Black women inform our work with students, colleagues, research, and our communities. Whereas normative theories and methods can fail to fully embody explanations of minoritized persons experiencing marginalization in the academy, using IM requires researchers to centralize Black women as the subject, enact critical lenses to uncover micro/macro power relations, acknowledge the role of power in the research process, and bring to the fore the complex identity markers operating in Black women's lives.

Thus, womanism, BFT, and IM hold promise in addressing the gap that
is rooted in Black women's experiences and penchant for reaching solutions that promote communal balance, affirm one's humanity and attend
to the spiritual dimension. Fostering inclusivity, acknowledged intersectionality, and communalist values, womanism offers scholars of color an
ethic of the embodied self. (Fraser-Burgess et al. 2021, 2)

Taking these frameworks together, then, has the potential to guide
the future study of ourselves and the impact of intersectional interventions, such as affinity group membership and support, on our early
career experiences in higher education. As such, intersectionality can
be used at the outset of a research project instead of being muted by
limiting it to a section in the literature review, theoretical framework,
or positionality statement.

While Black women's work and leadership have been discussed
in the extant literature on Black women's lives, the research usually
focuses on Black women faculty and staff in general (Burke, Cropper,
and Harrison 2000) or on Black women who hold high-level administration positions (Dillard 2016). As such, we present our stories as early
career Black women faculty to bear witness to the work we are paid to
do by contract; the work we are expected to do as department members,
program coordinators, dissertation advisors, and educational researchers; and the work we must do to meet the high expectations of Black
women's historical and intellectual excellence to which we subscribe.

Our experiences suggest the need for a thoughtful process to unpack
the work we are doing and the *work* we must do for our communities.
Further, we recognize that our exploration was made possible by the
lampposts left for us by Black women writers, historians, sociologists,
and researchers, and it is the pantheon of their wisdom that illuminates
our path as we have come to know the world thus far and as we begin
to understand the world of higher education.

In the final balance of our exploration, we say to Nanny: De [Black]
woman is *still* de mule uh de world so fur as *we* can see. But, Lawd!
Lawd! Lawd! We have agency, more models and frameworks that center and leverage Black women's work and experiences. We are using
better vehicles on the highways thrown up for our personal and professional success. We also have the power of rest and the power of no.

As evidenced by Black women's work before us and our current work, we also argue that there is no magic in the work we do. Black girl magic is needed, no doubt; but Black women's work will be how we convert that magic into the structural and systemic change required for the achievement and advancement of *all* of us and our children. And their children. And their children's children. And so it is.

REFERENCES

Allen, Evette L., and Nicole M. Joseph. 2018. "The Sistah Network: Enhancing the Educational and Social Experiences of Black Women in the Academy." *NASPA Journal About Women in Higher Education* 11, no. 2: 151–70.

Bloom, Harold, ed. 2008. *Zora Neale Hurston's Their Eyes Were Watching God.* New York: Infobase Publishing.

Burke, Beverley, Andrea Cropper, and Philomena Harrison. 2000. "Real or Imagined—Black Women's Experiences in the Academy." *Community, Work & Family* 3, no. 3: 297–310.

Croft, Sheryl, Miyoshi Juergensen, Tiffany D. Pogue, and Vincent Willis. 2018. "A Pedagogy of Intentionality: Developing Scholars Dedicated to Social Justice." *SoJo Journal: Educational Foundations and Social Justice Education* 4, no. 1: 31–43.

Dillard, Cynthia B. 2016. "To Address Suffering That the Majority Can't See: Lessons from Black Women's Leadership in the Workplace." *New Directions for Adult and Continuing Education* 2016, no. 152: 29–38.

Fraser-Burgess, Sheron Andrea, Kiesha Warren-Gordon, David L. Humphrey Jr., and Kendra Lowery. 2021. "Scholars of Color Turn to Womanism: Countering Dehumanization in the Academy." *Educational Philosophy and Theory* 53, no. 5: 505–22.

Haynes, Chayla, Nicole M. Joseph, Lori D. Patton, Saran Stewart, and Evette L. Allen. 2020. "Toward an Understanding of Intersectionality Methodology: A 30-Year Literature Synthesis of Black Women's Experiences in Higher Education." *Review of Educational Research* 90, no. 6: 751–87.

Hill Collins, Patricia. 2002. *Black Feminist Thought: Knowledge, Consciousness, and the Politics of Empowerment.* New York; London: Routledge.

June, Audrey. W., and Brian O'Leary. 2021. "How Many Black Women Have Tenure on Your Campus?" *The Chronicle of Higher Education* 27.

Ladson-Billings, Gloria. 1995. "Toward a Theory of Culturally Relevant Pedagogy." *American Educational Research Journal* 32, no. 3: 465–91.

Shaw, Stephanie J. 1996. *What a Woman Ought to Be and to Do.* Chicago: University of Chicago Press.

Souto-Manning, Mariana, and Nichole Ray. 2007. "Beyond Survival in the Ivory Tower: Black and Brown Women's Living Narratives." *Equity & Excellence in Education* 40, no. 4: 280–90.

Walker, Alice. (1983) 2004. *In Search of Our Mothers' Gardens: Womanist Prose.* Orlando, FL: Harcourt.

CHAPTER 6

Lost and Found
A Tale of Two Black Women Seeking Solidarity within Academia
Erica-Brittany Horhn and Sharon Lassiter

"I ONCE WAS LOST"

Black women have often felt isolated and excluded from academic, professional, and social life. To combat this exclusion, Black women in the late 1800s created their own sister circles, support groups specifically for Black women to discuss, and at times lament on, their various lived experiences. These sister circles set the foundation for the Black Women's Club Movement, igniting a stronger sense of agency and Black women's empowerment (Giddings 2007).

Today, while Black women have more access and opportunity, many still suffer from isolation and exclusion, particularly as they matriculate through doctoral programs. In *Teaching to Transgress*, hooks (2017) exclaims that she came to theory because she was hurting; likewise, Black women in academia are hurting as they experience racism, sexism, and ageism, in addition to navigating work-life balance, networking, and preparation for an academic workforce when applicable. Despite these challenges, Black women continue to enter into and complete doctoral programs. To maneuver within and beyond the confines of academia, Black women continue seeking solidarity and finding solace among each other.

Borne out of the need for two Black woman scholars to better understand their experiences in the academy, the Retaining Each Other Framework (Fries-Britt and Kelly 2005) highlights personal connection as a means for Black women to survive academia. Fries-Britt and Kelly's friendship both sustained them and retained them within their academic careers. The Retaining Each Other Framework expands research rooted in understanding Black women's solidarity and belonging to include peer mentoring, sister circles, and other Black-women-led affinity groups (Minnett, James-Gallaway, and Owens 2019; Winkle-Wagner et al. 2019).

To further expand on this framework, the authors use critical auto-ethnography (CAE)—a qualitative methodological approach that "empowers researchers to engage in a collective examination of individual autobiographies to understand a sociocultural phenomenon" (Ashlee, Zamora, and Karikar 2017, 91)—to analyze their own experiences navigating doctoral programs and the ways their intergenerational sister circle contributed to their academic success. The work presented here is rooted in the narrative elements of critical autoethnography in which, "the life experiences of the anthropologist and their relationships with others 'in the field' should be interrogated and explored" (Reed-Danahay 2017, 144). The choice to let their stories speak for themselves is in line with the existing research that celebrates Black voices in knowledge creation even when they are not recognized by traditional research (Evans-Winters and Love 2015). It is the authors' hope that their collaborative piece provokes a more nuanced way of exploring intergenerational sister circles.

DANIELLE'S STORY

Danielle's family instilled the importance of education early, and like most parents, they supported her in all her endeavors. During most of her educational years, she attended Historically White Institutions (HWIs), where she learned early how to navigate White educational spaces. Danielle received her master's degree from a large Historically Black College/University (HBCU), and it was the first time she was not the minority in the classroom. She appreciated the professors' attentiveness. Under their tutelage, she gained more confidence in her intellect and was affirmed by her peers in ways she had not been at previous institutions. While Danielle grew academically, she still relied mostly on herself to make it through the program.

When it came time to complete doctoral work, Danielle excelled in the classroom but struggled on her own. Her family wanted to help, but because she was the first to continue her education to this degree, they could not. A male friend and student of color recognized Danielle's troubles and asked if she needed a mentor. He arranged a dinner meeting with an older woman from a neighboring HBCU, where Danielle received her master's degree.

At dinner they discussed research interests, committee members, and her future goals. After giving a few general tips on how to navigate the program, she asked Danielle what she needed in a mentor. She was the first person Danielle encountered who explicitly talked to her about mentorship. Up until that point, Danielle never knew she needed a mentor. While the woman at dinner never did become her mentor, she made Danielle aware of her own blind spots and her need to ask for help. This became especially important after her coursework, when she longed for classroom interactions.

Danielle and Renee met through a mutual friend. They exchanged numbers and began going on small restaurant outings, where they laughed together and shared stories about work and school. Their sister circle formed organically. This was the mentorship Danielle needed in a space that felt authentic. Without Renee's friendship and her consistent willingness to share space, Danielle would not have survived her PhD journey.

RENEE'S STORY

Renee learned from her upbringing that education was a profitable tool that afforded African Americans from poor, rural communities the chance to advance in their careers and improve their financial circumstances. As a child, Renee developed a passion for learning from conversations with her great uncle, who served as a college professor at an illustrious HBCU. As a young adult, she witnessed her mother's drive to earn an associate's degree in business administration because her mother saw it as her way to leverage her leadership opportunities at the textile mill where she worked.

During her K–12 schooling, Renee was fortunate enough to have school leaders and teachers who recognized her academic potential beyond her standardized test scores. They placed Renee in advanced-level learning groups and in positions of student leadership. However, her test scores on college entrance exams had narrowed the pool of universities for which she met the application criteria. Renee applied to one university, a Historically White Institution, and made the decision to attend because they were the first to accept her. However, after one semester, Renee transferred to the local HBCU because the Historically White Institution lacked the educational nurturing that she benefitted from during her K–12 experiences in her predominantly Black schools.

In 2002, Renee took another blow to her self-efficacy from her performance on a standardized graduate school admittance exam. A HWI denied her entry into its doctor of philosophy program focused on curriculum and instruction, solely based on her quantitative reasoning scores on the standardized admittance exam. After nearly two decades, Renee was accepted into a doctor of philosophy program focused on leadership. It was the same HBCU from which she had already received one undergraduate and two graduate degrees.

Unlike her previous postsecondary studies at the HBCU, the self-paced nature of the dissertation phase of the doctoral program led Renee to forge an academic sisterhood not only with Black females in her doctoral program but also with Black females in a doctoral program at the nearby HWI that had rejected her decades earlier. Both academic sister circles immensely contributed to Renee's navigation on her doctoral journey; however, this chapter will focus on Renee's membership in the one in which she was the outsider.

HAVING A SEAT AT THE TABLE: A GLIMPSE INTO THE SISTER CIRCLE WORK PARTY

To capture Danielle and Renee's experiences as Black women in doctoral programs, the findings are presented as a scholarly narrative because as Evans-Winters and Love (2015) suggest, "Taking on a dialogical voice, the act of listening, writing, and conversing grounded in one's cultural point of reference, in the design and pursuit of knowledge, is a result of the Black women's lived experiences in communal and civic space" (136).

Formatting the findings as a conversation between friends allows for a more authentic depiction of their friendship and uncovers the ways they supported each other through their intergenerational sister circle. Though their sister circle included other women, they were the only ones to complete their respective doctoral programs. The following interview discusses three themes: (1) questioning self and establishing trust, (2) navigating racialized spaces, and (3) experiences as outsiders inside their academic sisterhood.

Questioning Self and Establishing Trust

Black female doctoral student seeking solidarity (BFDS): Self-efficacy seems to be a common theme among your stories. What role did this play in your ability to establish trust within your academic sisterhood?

Danielle: A colleague once told me, a doctoral program is not for the faint of heart. For me the politics of the program was difficult to manage. Our sister circle work parties came at a time when I was most unsure of myself personally and academically. I was not getting much guidance within the program, and for the first time, I didn't know how to help myself. The moments of being in limbo really shook my confidence. My lack of confidence in the actual academic process led to a lack of confidence in my intellectual abilities.

Renee: It is quite interesting that Danielle attributed both her high school and academy experiences to how she navigated the doctoral program. Truthfully, I found her scholarly experiences at HWIs intimidating. My rejection from the HWI's doctoral program left an indelible mark on my scholarly capacity and guided my initial engagement in the academic sisterhood. The blow to my self-efficacy had left me doubting my ability to be of value at the dissertation-writing parties. There was genuine surprise when Danielle asked for feedback on her writing ideas, but it also confirmed that trust had been established within the academic sisterhood. Additionally, it alleviated my apprehensions of scholarly writing; it affirmed my belonging in a doctoral program. Trust is the foundation of building solidarity within an academic sisterhood. Trust leads to the vulnerability that is needed within this sisterhood for one to grow as a dissertation scholar within the academy.

Both Danielle's and Renee's K–20 academic experiences shook their academic confidence. The academic sisterhood gifted them with the intellectual affirmation for which they longed. Their sister circle work party was a space where they could openly express their academic deficiencies, which ultimately forced them to be vulnerable enough to ask for help with things they did not know and to make corrections. This ultimately helped in their productivity.

Fries-Britt and Kelly (2005) describe the moment in the sister circle as "not only freeing and liberating but it move[s] us along in the writing process because we could identify where and when we needed help" (221–22). This process motivated Danielle and Renee to push through the respective challenges. While Danielle and Renee successfully matriculated through their programs, they were the only ones in the sister circle to do so.

Navigating Racialized Spaces

BFDS: You both obtained undergraduate and graduate degrees from racialized institutions. What was it like for you to navigate those postsecondary racialized spaces?

Danielle: I guess you could say that I am the product of both an HWI and an HBCU, but I know my high school and college HWI experiences have shaped the way I navigated my doctoral program. I was always taught that I needed to work twice as hard because of my race and my gender. This meant that I kept my head down and continued to do my work. It definitely taught me to perform academics a particular way.

During most of my formative education years, I attended HWIs, and I was often the only Black student in class, or in the whole institution for that matter. I did not have the language of microaggressions, but I recognized differential treatment. When my teachers posted final grades and I was one of the higher grades, I recognized the looks of confusion, and for the bold students, I answered questions like "How did you do that?" or I overheard questions like "Are you sure the grades are right?" Navigating this space meant learning to rely on myself and become academically resourceful. The HWIs I attended celebrated independent work and individual achievement. Collaboration with faculty was encouraged, but collaboration among students was rare.

Renee: It was not easy learning to access the academic support and resources at the HWI. Like Danielle, working in isolation became the norm; yet, unlike Danielle, a lack of courage and the fear of failure drove this sister's decision to transfer. The local HBCU was familiar. In *this* racialized space was my best friend from high school, who acclimated me to the university. In *this* racialized space was consistent support from professors and peers. My professors prepared me for what was to come, such as the professor who told us that the day would come when we would have to learn to walk alone on our dissertation journey.

In *this* racialized space was a collaborative spirit that prepared me to seek out academic sisterhoods to not only survive but also overcome the struggles of a doctoral program. Walking alone was not an option when learning as a collective had been instrumental to my postsecondary success. Seeking solidarity within an academic sisterhood during the dissertation-writing phase of the doctoral program filled the peer support void that my professor had warned me about, but that I was unwilling to accept.

Danielle: I'll be the first to say that early on, I was the more rigid one in the work party. While some of that was because I was on a hard deadline to finish, most of it was because in the past, collaboration meant that I did the work, and someone else received credit. I learned early that group work environments were not for me. I was there to work and check off things on my to-do list!

I will say, though, that working with this group was different. It was the first time I felt that I could contribute and learn from the group. There was a mutual exchange that was not always present in previous environments. To use your words, Renee, I was used to walking alone, but at the writing stage of the program, walking alone was too isolating. Working in this sister circle with you made me come out of my comfort zone.

Their stories highlight the challenges within their educational journeys. Danielle's and Renee's responses show a direct connection between *where* they were educated and *how* they navigated racialized academic spaces. Renee's formative college years at an HBCU consisted of preparing her for life beyond the academy. Danielle, on the other hand, had always experienced what was to come from her HWI in the form of independent work and academic isolation. With the dissertation phase of their programs came academic isolation. Just as

Teasdell and colleagues (2021) suggest, they both desired collaborative academic support that would push them toward the finish line.

Their personal and academic experiences within both types of racialized academic spaces shaped their engagement in their academic sisterhood. When working toward an academic relationship, their educational preparation also influenced how they learned to trust each other. But first they had to learn to trust and accept the knowledge they possessed even when it was not valued within their respective programs.

Outsiders Inside the Academic Sisterhood

BFDS: Aside from being enrolled in doctoral programs at two different racialized spaces, what other differences influenced your experiences within your academic sisterhood?

Danielle: Within our group, there were age differences. I believe we are fourteen years apart. At times when you discussed things that I had not experienced yet, I knew to listen. I was an outsider in the group because of my age, but because we shared a cultural connection and a shared educational experience, I still had a limited insider perspective. I could still laugh along with your stories about marriage. At one point, we built a relationship where we could tease each other about age and other things.

Renee: There was definitely a noticeable generational difference. As the oldest member in the sisterhood, there was concern of not being accepted. Although Danielle was fourteen years my junior, we had more in common than we initially realized. The shared values and mindsets made it easy for the writing parties to become the therapeutic moments that I needed to keep from quitting. The academic sisterhood provided me with listening ears, sage advice, and an abundance of laughter. However, it was the difference in racialized spaces that influenced my experience the most.

As previously stated, Danielle's experiences in White academic spaces was intimidating. I had entered this academic sisterhood thinking I was too dumb to work with Danielle, and that she would discover that I was an interloper and an imposter. I thought that Danielle would perceive that I did not belong in the scholarly circle and was an academic fraud. Yet bonding over commonalities beyond being Black female scholars helped to nurture our friendship; that became more powerful than our generational and racialized spaces differences. For example, conversations emerged about shared experiences in a master's degree program at the local HBCU that created a sense of belonging within our academic sisterhood. Additionally, there was bonding over humorous stories we shared about our lived experiences outside of academia.

Danielle: We all suffer from imposter syndrome at some point in these programs. I never knew you were intimidated by my experiences. If anything, *I* was intimidated by *your* experiences outside of the academy. You were established in your career and intentional about the choice of doctoral program and the courses you took in ways I was not. At times I reverted back to my survival technique: performing academics in ways that hid my insecurities, namely being quiet about my own insecurities and focusing on the tasks. Your patience and genuine interest in me and my research allowed me to be vulnerable in sharing the good and bad parts of my PhD journey. I didn't have to hide behind intellect the way I did when I was younger. We're peers despite our age difference!

Danielle and Renee found their identities as intergenerational Black female scholars to be value-added to their doctoral journey. These intersecting identities created the opportunity for them to learn more about each other academically, professionally, and personally. Their outsider status, based on age, did not hinder them in developing a friendship beyond their academic sister circle.

Beyond academics, they discovered similar tastes in food and music. They took an interest in each other's families and slowly became staples in each other's lives. They later became sorority sisters, where they continued to celebrate their personal and professional achievements. Jones and Osborne-Lampkin (2013) suggest that these multiple identities presented the opportunity for understanding, accepting, and validating their shared experiences as doctoral students.

"AND NOW I'M FOUND"

Black women doctoral students of all ages exist in the academy serving as symbols of survival, resistance, and strength (Wallace et al. 2020, 7). While Danielle's and Renee's accounts reinforce the existing literature on the importance of sister circles and Black women's success, they also open up possibilities for additional research on Black intergenerational friendships in higher-education spaces and beyond. Sharing Danielle's and Renee's stories as Black female doctoral students seeking belonging in the academy reinforces the work of Patterson-Stephens and Hernandez (2018), as the sister circle developed Danielle's and Renee's socialization not only as doctoral researchers but also as future tenure-track professors. Their experience suggests that despite self-imposed and institutional barriers, Black women at both HWIs and HBCUs must continue to be academically resourceful in order to matriculate through doctoral programs.

Sister circles are a vital resource for Black women in doctoral programs. They assist in building solidarity through engaging in an academic sisterhood that fills specific voids in one's program. Danielle's and Renee's experiences demonstrate two salient best practices for a rewarding sister circle: (1) reaching across disciplines, across age, and across institutions to sustain oneself, and (2) building relationships grounded in trust and transparency.

REFERENCES

Ashlee, Aeriel A., Bianca Zamora, and Shamika N Karikari. 2017. "We Are Woke: A Collaborative Critical Autoethnography of Three 'Womxn' of Color Graduate Students in Higher Education." *International Journal of Multicultural Education* 19, no. 1: 89.

Evans-Winters, Venus E., and Bettina L. Love, eds. 2015. *Black Feminism in Education: Black Women Speak Back, Up, and Out.* New York: Peter Lang.

Fries-Britt, Sharon, and Bridget Turner Kelly. 2005. "Retaining Each Other: Narratives of Two African American Women in the Academy." *The Urban Review* 37, no. 3: 221–42.

Giddings Paula J. 2007. *When and Where I Enter: The Impact of Black Women on Race and Sex in America.* New York: HarperCollins.

hooks, bell. 2017. *Teaching to Transgress: Education as the Practice of Freedom.* New York: Routledge.

Jones, Tamara B., and La'Tara Osborne-Lampkin. 2013. "Black Female Faculty Success and Early Career Professional Development." *The Negro Educational Review* 64, nos. 1–4: 59–135.

Minnett, Jari L., ArCasia D. James-Gallaway, and Devean R. Owens. 2019. "Help a Sista Out: Black Women Doctoral Students' Use of Peer Mentorship as an Act of Resistance." *Mid-Western Educational Researcher* 31, no. 2.

Patterson-Stephens, Shawna, and Estee Hernández. 2018. "Hermandad: Sista' Scholar Bonds for Black and Chicana Women in Doctoral Study." *Equity & Excellence in Education* 51, no. 3–4: 396–415.

Reed-Danahay, Deborah. 2017. "Bourdieu and Critical Autoethnography: Implications for Research, Writing, and Teaching," *International Journal of Multicultural Education* 19, no. 1: 144.

Teasdell, Annette, Shanique Lee, Alexis Calloway, and Tempestt Adams. 2021. "Commitment, Community, Consciousness: A Collaborative Autoethnography of a Doctoral Sister Circle." *Journal of African American Women and Girls in Education* 1, no. 1: 7–23.

Wallace, Erica R., Carla Cadet Fullwood, Erica-Brittany Horhn, Camaron Loritts, Brandy S. Propst, and Coretta Roseboro Walker. 2020. "The Black Feminist Mixtape: A Collective Black Feminist Autoethnography of Black Women's Existence in the Academy." *Journal of Critical Scholarship on Higher Education and Student Affairs* 5, no. 3: 7.

Winkle-Wagner, Rachelle, Bridget Turner Kelly, Courtney L. Luedke, and Tangela Blakely Reavis. 2019, April. "Authentically Me: Examining Expectations That Are Placed upon Black Women in College." *American Educational Research Journal* 56, no. 2: 407–43.

CHAPTER 7

From Clinical to Tenure-Track Faculty
Scholarly Reflections of Teaching and Learning
Joy L. Kennedy

The National Center for Education Statistics (2020) reports that 1.5 million faculty members are employed in public and private degree-granting colleges/universities in the United States. These statistics include part- and full-time faculty with designated academic ranks as adjunct (or interim), instructor, lecturer, assistant professor, associate professor, and professor. Of the 1.5 million faculty members, individuals reported race and/or ethnicity classifications as White (75 percent), Black (6 percent), Hispanic (6 percent), Asian/Pacific Islander (12 percent), American Indian/Alaska Native (1 percent), and two or more races (1 percent).

Furthermore, in terms of gender, 53 percent of faculty identified as males, and 46 percent identified as females. Although there is a 7 percent difference between the employment statistics of male and female faculty members, a notable difference is evident among the race and ethnicity classifications of faculty, with a dominant presence of White males (40 percent) and White females (35 percent) across all academic ranks. Consequently, these statistics emphasize a significant need for faculty who identify as Black, Indigenous, Persons of Color (BIPOC) within postsecondary institutions.

The author, who identifies as a Black woman, realized the need for BIPOC faculty while completing degree requirements for a PhD in educational studies with a concentration in cultural studies. After graduation, the author was presented with a faculty employment opportunity for a clinical assistant professor position at a Historically White Institution (HWI). Five years later, the author transitioned to a Historically Black College/University (HBCU) in a tenure-track, assistant professor faculty position. Therefore, this chapter will provide insight about clinical and academic faculty positions in the potential recruitment of BIPOC faculty.

CLINICAL FACULTY

Clinical education is an integral component of most education (teacher-education/preparation programs), medical (physicians, nursing, and dental), and allied health (social work, speech-language pathology, audiology, occupational therapy, physical therapy, etc.) professions in the preparation of pre-professionals to work in educational and medical settings. The common practice for most undergraduate and/or graduate programs is the differentiation of clinical and academic coursework. Thus, clinical faculty positions are typically fixed-term or non-tenure-track positions with an emphasis in clinical teaching.

The teaching duties of clinical faculty can include working with students either individually or in small groups in the facilitation of pre-session and debriefing meetings, technique modeling, observations, review of reports/paperwork, and mentoring. Nevertheless, clinical faculty, ultimately, facilitate the preparation of pre-professionals to work with people (students, clients, patients) from culturally and linguistically diverse backgrounds. Although clinical education is often relegated to clinical practicum fieldwork, teaching students how to interact with diverse groups of persons can occur within academic coursework too.

For instance, Osmond et al. (2012) developed an interdisciplinary undergraduate course titled Narrative and the Caring Professions for pre-medical, pre-dental, nursing, social work, and education students (1). The objectives of the course include using literature, memoirs, and poetry to facilitate conversations about the human dimensions of care-giving that are interrelated with the diverse cultural and social needs of people (1). This course is a creative example of how to utilize course discussions and materials that will engage students in the understanding of professional care skills for generalization in clinical practicum courses and fieldwork.

Furthermore, Osmond et al. (2012) have utilized grant funding to develop the course as a group for one year (1). Similarly, most postsecondary institutions will encourage clinical faculty to engage in research for academic-rank promotions. Research activities can include being a principal investigator, writing publications/grants, and completing presentations, but they are typically given the lowest workload percentage for clinical faculty among other designated duties. As a result, the completion of research activities can be burdensome for clinical faculty, who are not provided support in workload-distribution expectations.

Nevertheless, it is not impossible for clinical faculty to be actively engaged in teaching and research activities. Several clinical faculty members have successfully integrated clinical education/teaching activities as research projects with undergraduate and/or graduate students. In particular, the author facilitated case studies of clients/patients with clinical practicum students that resulted in conference presentations. Students reported appreciating the opportunity to engage in clinical research that enhanced their professional development as pre-professionals.

Moreover, the clinical research activities enabled the author to serve as a mentor to undergraduate and graduate students. One of the author's mentoring goals incorporates advising students about the clinical faculty positions as an informal pipeline recruitment approach, especially with BIPOC students, to working in colleges and universities. Furthermore, the author informs students of degree and employment requirements that are not broadly advertised for both clinical and tenure-track faculty positions.

TENURE-TRACK FACULTY

Similar to clinical faculty positions, tenure-track faculty positions are comprised of teaching, research, and service duties. The one major difference is that tenure-track faculty positions place a significant emphasis on research activities, and obtaining tenure is often referred to as the *publish or perish* process. As mentioned previously, research activities can include manuscript writing for journal/book publications, grant writing for funding opportunities, conference presentations, mentoring of student research projects, interprofessional research collaborations, and implementation and/or facilitation of research projects.

James (2014) provides an analogy of tenure-track faculty positions being like a *game* that has rules, losers, and winners (5). A primary rule that tenure-track faculty should be more concerned with is building the curriculum vitae (CV) through research publications (13). For the research publications to be considered as significant research contributions during tenure review, the manuscripts need to be either published or in press for publication (40). Ultimately, the goal for tenure-track faculty should involve proving their research credibility among other senior researchers in their chosen research topic, which will provide other funding and employment opportunities (13).

Though this explanation of research activities as a major responsibility for tenure-track faculty seems reasonable, the tasks of teaching, service, and advising commitments can be time consuming and decrease research productivity, particularly for first- or second-year junior faculty. Sligh Dewalt (2006), who provides personal insight of the tenure-track process as a Black female at an HBCU, describes the usefulness of expressing a "political no" to achieve research productivity for the tenure-track timeline (140). As Sligh Dewalt (2006) writes, "As a first year [tenure-track] faculty member, if you do not say no to certain things, you may experience 'the dump'" (140). This "dump" can include being recruited to teach summer courses and for numerous service committees/commitments that can ultimately hinder personal time and energy toward the tenure-track process (140). Additionally, academic advising is another obligation that can be time consuming for tenure-track faculty. For instance, although the author enjoys mentoring students and being student friendly, academic advising has been a "dump" tenure-track experience.

Even though advising can be a rewarding experience for both the advisee and advisor, the author acknowledges the need to establish boundaries with scheduling too many additional meetings with students and always being available for communication via email. If not monitored, these extra student-friendly duties can interfere with research productivity too. Therefore, learning to say "no" to students and faculty will be crucial for tenure-track faculty, especially BIPOC faculty in either HBCU or HWI work environments.

HBCUS VERSUS HWIS

The historic purpose and student populations of HBCUs and HWIs are implied in the respective terms, with majority Black/African American students attending HBCUs and majority White/Caucasian students attending HWIs. As a result, BIPOC faculty members who choose to work in either setting should be intentional in research, teaching, and service activities that promote the inclusion of culturally and linguistically diverse topics that are often marginalized in mainstream academic settings.

Lee (2006), as a Navajo woman faculty member, has engaged her marginalized positionality within the center of teaching, research, and service to support her presence and purpose in the college/university (50). Lee also conveys desiring to not lose her identity and being concerned "about judging [herself] from a White person's perspective" (50). To maintain personal identity, Lee became a faculty member in the Native American Studies Department at the University of New Mexico, an institution with students of color as the majority population. Therefore, Lee remained conscious of personal and communal reasons in the education and recruitment of Native American students to pursue doctoral degrees at the university (50).

Likewise, similar to Lee, when determining a postsecondary setting of employment, potential faculty members should understand the primary student population and the founding historical implications of the college or university. Even though institutions such as HBCUs and HWIs have different majority student populations, faculty members will usually interact with diverse groups of students in either setting. The diversity can be attributed to race/ethnicity, gender identity, social class, religion preference, lived experiences, and so forth. In most instances, students are not encouraged to examine their multiple identities that can be marginalized in mainstream and academic settings.

A method that facilitates the centering of marginalized identities, either individually or within groups, is "intersectionality" (Hill Collins and Bilge 2016, 31). The definition of *intersectionality* states, "Intersectionality is a way of understanding and analyzing the complexities of the world, in people, and in human experiences" (Hill Collins and Bilge 2016, 2). Additionally, intersectional analysis occurs through the investigations of social divisions (race, gender, class), structural power relationships, privilege, and practice (Hill Collins and Bilge 2016, 2). Thus, two key components of intersectional scholarship are critical inquiry and critical praxis (Hill Collins and Bilge 2016, 31).

Faculty at HBCUs or HWIs can facilitate critical inquiry through the investigation of cultural and social standards. For instance, in educational, allied health, and medical fields, faculty members can lead discussions about the implications of mainstream English and dialect speakers. The conversation can probe the misdiagnosis of dialect speakers with language-learning disorders or communication disorders. Furthermore, an analysis of how language and dialect may influence the understanding of health communication information can be vital problem-solving information for pre-professional students.

The second component of intersectionality, critical praxis, expands on critical inquiry through the problem-solving of social problems. As an example, faculty and students can examine the relationships between illiteracy and poverty rates of dialect speakers that typically exacerbate violence, homelessness, and hunger issues. These matters can then be analyzed in relationship to institutional structures that support or impede the quality of life of dialect speakers. Critical praxis is more than conversation for mere conversation: "Critical praxis is an important analytical strategy for doing social justice" (Hill Collins and Bilge 2016, 42).

The mission of most colleges and universities includes a component of service that is social justice motivated within local communities. Thus, conversations about social-justice matters using intersectional frameworks should be facilitated by faculty members at both HBCUs and HWIs. Ultimately, being employed at either an HBCU or HWI is a matter of choice for faculty members, who should seek to have a primary focus on the inclusivity of diverse topics and perspectives in their teaching, research, and service.

There is a significant need for BIPOC faculty in public and private degree-granting colleges and universities. Clinical faculty positions offer opportunities primarily in teaching and service with some research responsibilities. Tenure-track faculty positions are heavily focused on research activities, teaching, and service. Both clinical and tenure-track faculty positions are typically available in the education, allied health, nursing, and medical fields. BIPOC faculty should choose a college or university for employment in alignment with personal and institutional social-justice missions on campus and in the local community.

Since the author's doctorate degree has an emphasis in cultural studies, the author is passionate about the inclusion of culturally and linguistically diverse topics in clinical and academic courses. As a clinical educator at an HWI, the author integrated topics pertaining to not only race/ethnicity but also social class status, religion, and gender identity with undergraduate and graduate students. Likewise, as tenure-track faculty at an HBCU, the author includes the same culturally and linguistically diverse topics because undergraduate students of color are also diverse in their personal experiences and understanding of culture.

Having a foundational framework of culture relative to one's personal experiences and other people is essential for students and professionals in education, medical, and allied health fields. While the author has experienced moments of being overwhelmed with the numerous responsibilities in the higher-education system within the HWI and HBCU settings, the author's desire to facilitate the preparation of culturally competent professionals has been paramount to her continued presence in academia.

REFERENCES

Hill Collins, Patricia, and Sirma Bilge. 2016. *Intersectionality.* Cambridge, UK; Malden, MA: Polity Press.

James, Russell. 2014. *Tenure Hacks: The 12 Secrets of Making Tenure.* N.p.: CreateSpace.

Lee, Tiffany S. 2006. "Balancing the Margin Is My Center: A Navajo Woman's Navigations through the Academy and Her Community." In *From Oppression to Grace: Women of Color and Their Dilemmas within the Academy,* edited by Theodorea Regina Berry and Nathalie D. Mizelle, 44–58. N.p.: Stylus.

National Center for Education Statistics. 2020. "Fast Facts: Race/Ethnicity of College Faculty." https://nces.ed.gov/fastfacts/display.asp?id=61.

Osmond, Chris, Sharon Ann Cumbie, Michael Dale, David Hostetler, James Ivory, Deborah Phillips, and Karen Reesman. 2012. "An Open Letter to Our Future Students in 'Narrative and the Caring Professions.'" *Journal for Learning through the Arts* 8, no. 1: 1–7.

Sligh DeWalt, Cassandra. 2006. "Sides of the Tenure and Promotion Process: Can I Be a Parental Figure, Scholar and Spouse?" In *From Oppression to Grace: Women of Color and Their Dilemmas within the Academy*, edited by Theodorea Regina Berry and Nathalie D. Mizelle, 138–46. N.p.: Stylus.

Part III

MENTORSHIP OR SPONSORSHIP

Engineer or Test Pilot
Naming and Claiming a Successful Mentoring Relationship
Yolanda F. Holt

In 1999, Dolores Battle published the article "Retention of Minority Faculty in Higher Education." In the text, Battle (1999) identifies six complex and interrelated issues in the retention of minority faculty:

1. leaving to take positions at other universities;
2. overwork in committee service;
3. lack of support and encouragement;
4. putting minority faculty on display (as evidence of diversity);
5. faculty concern regarding the ability to achieve tenure; and
6. campus climate.

In the two decades since this article was published, little has changed. A recent study on the recruitment and retention of Black faculty at Historically White Institutions by Edwards and Ross (2018) reveals Black faculty members share a similar list of concerns. The top three issues were, again, a lack of mentors (consistent with lack of support and encouragement from Battle's [1999] findings), lack of transparency in the tenure and promotion process, and limited guidance for tenure and promotion (both consistent with faculty concern regarding the ability to achieve tenure from Battle [1999]).

The consistency of these experiences of Black faculty members across institutions of higher learning in two different decades suggests the academic institution has made limited progress in improving the experience of Black faculty in the academy. Yet the number of Black people, particularly Black women, earning PhDs continues to increase. However, success in the academy, in the Ivory Tower, requires more than increasing the number of Black individuals with PhDs. Once the academic degree is achieved, the individual must showcase their academic pedigree. That is, the individual must connect the dots from the work and the structured interactions acquired during their graduate and dissertation process to their current well-earned faculty status to the yet-uncharted research and scholarship promised land.

However, as many, though not all, Black, underrepresented minority and women faculty are not just first-generation PhDs, but also first-generation college students, they may lack access to the resources and knowledge for the success in this process. For these individuals, a broad understanding of the path to tenure and promotion is not enough. These scholars are experiencing every aspect of their journey as a first experience with no handbook and no guide. This chapter is written with that scholar in mind, those who know they do not know and yet have no idea what they should know. This group of scholars may need both mentorship and/or sponsorship at varying points in their professional pursuits. This text will provide a brief look at the development and implementation of mentoring and sponsoring relationships from the perspective of that scholar.

First, this chapter will define *mentorship* and *sponsorship*, followed by a description of how to create mentoring relationships through networking, scholarly presentations, and developing social relationships. The final section will discuss how to leverage mentoring relationships to sponsorships or how to get people to elevate your name when you are not in the room. The chapter will end with steps to take to develop a network of mentors and advocate for sponsorship. With this process in mind, you are asked to consider whether you are currently engaging with the academy as a test pilot, relying on the work and goodwill of others to navigate the dynamic tenure and promotion process, or as an engineer, positively engaging with peers and senior faculty and speaking to your own strengths before describing your needs.

THE RULES CAN BE BENT, BUT YOU MUST KNOW THE RULES: EXPECTATIONS AND RECIPROCITY IN THE ACADEMY

There are several definitions of *mentoring* and *sponsoring*. In this chapter, the term *mentoring* refers to broad career-focused support provided to an individual. This definition is a modification of the traditional definition, such as the one given by Cao and Yang (2013), who define mentoring as the career and psychosocial developmental support provided by a senior person (mentor) to a junior person (protégé). The purpose of modifying Cao and Yang's (2013) definition is to expand readers' thinking about mentorship from a one-on-one senior-to-junior relationship to a network of peer-to-peer knowledge transmission and the development of a communication and sharing network for career advancement. This definition differs from the traditional mentoring relationship of a junior being guided by a more knowledgeable senior, as defined by Cao and Yang (2013).

There are three problems with the traditional mentoring model in cross-cultural relationships for protégés who identify as women and people of color. First, there can be a mismatch between the knowledge, skills, and expectations between the protégé and the mentor. Mentors from majority cultures may not be aware of or take seriously cultural differences in non-majority cultural approaches to learning, communication, and feedback. This cultural mismatch for a minority protégé to a majority mentor can result in miscommunication and friction within the mentoring relationship that is a mirror of the miscommunication and friction that drew the protégé to seek mentoring.

A second issue is the unspoken cultural expectation of a majority mentor with no or limited training in cross-cultural communication. Due to their longevity in the university or the field, the mentor is expected to have knowledge of what the protégé needs to know or needs to do for success. Even with frequent, open, and frank discussions regarding the protégé's goals and expectations, the interactions and outcomes of a minority protégé may be quite different from those experienced by the majority mentor. This can be due to societal expectations for what the protégé could or should be doing/able to do. In this instance, the cultural experiences of the mentor may not have prepared them to deal with the obstacles faced by the protégé. This is no one's fault but is a cultural fault line that remains for the protégé to navigate. A culturally untrained mentor may be ill equipped to support the needs of their protégé.

Finally, there may be a mismatch between the cultural expectations for professional interactions between the pair. The mentor may expect behaviors that the protégé does not perform. The protégé's failure to perform the unwritten expectations may be viewed as a lack of fit instead of a simple lack of cultural expectations. An example of this is the discipline-specific order of authors on a scholarly manuscript. In some disciplines, the senior author's name appears first, in others last. The protégé's level of knowledge in this area may be read as a lack of academic preparation, not a lack of cultural knowledge. Similarly, the unwritten rules of mentorship in the academy add an additional layer of need for cross-cultural understanding. Unfortunately, that burden for cross-cultural understanding is most frequently born by the protégé.

Two alternatives to the traditional one-on-one mentor-protégé dynamic are peer-to-peer or near-to-peer mentoring with multiple individuals. The near-to-peer and peer-to-peer mentoring dynamics are an expansion of the hierarchical one-on-one pairings of a senior to a junior faculty member. The near-to-peer model can be structured as group-based mentoring and mentoring networks designed to meet the complex needs experienced by the new faculty member (Willingham-McLain, Margolis, and Klingler 2019). Near peers are early career faculty with two to four years of experience of recent success navigating the complex organizational and institutional pathways the new faculty member will encounter. Both the early career faculty and the new faculty member benefit from engaging in the near-to-peer mentoring process.

The successful early career faculty member assists the new faculty in connecting with the university structures in a broad, encompassing manner. The near-to-peer mentor can assist the new hire in understanding and navigating the institutional practices and organizational structure of the university. Due to their recent experience with the process, the near-to-peer mentor and the new hire are likely to develop reciprocal and horizontal mentoring. The individuals are learning from each other (Willingham-McLain et al. 2019), as they both gain greater understanding of the promotion and tenure process. This process is particularly instructive in near-to-peer group mentoring, where individuals from a variety of college units are part of the mentoring cohort. The primary negative associated with this form of mentorship is scheduling a common time for small-group meetings.

Near-to-peer mentoring is beneficial not just for early career faculty. Friberg et al. (2021) describe the importance of validating the mentoring relationships that emerge from unexpected interactions among senior scholars as they build reciprocally beneficial relationships within disciplines of study. Naming and claiming is the process of identifying and describing the emerging needs for, and opportunities to, provide mentorship between near peers. The authors suggest this form of mentorship should be recognized for its benefits and promoted as a legitimate and valuable form of mentoring. For mid-career and senior faculty, near-to-peer mentoring may derive from shared interests in research and scholarship.

Similar in construct to near-to-peer mentoring, peer-to-peer mentoring is described by Morton and Gil (2019) as a collective model of mentorship that leverages group support to work toward group rather than individual success. A primary feature of this form of mentoring is decentralization and flattening of the mentor-protégé relationship, expanding the unitary relationship in favor of a co-constructed peer-mentoring model. For underrepresented minorities, such a collective is beneficial along multiple parameters.

The women described by Morton and Gil (2019) benefited from the community support of women at the same early career and life stage. The cohort of underrepresented minority women benefited from having a shared point of view in understanding the common barriers to success in the academy. The peers developed personal and professional relationships during the mentoring process, an antidote to the typically competitive nature of academia (Benishek et al. 2004; Karam et al. 2012).

This collective and organized support system allowed the faculty to engage in academic pursuits in a manner that aligned with their cultural belief system (Morton and Gil 2019). The members further benefited from the exposure to each other's expertise as they developed writing and research collaborations across disciplinary boundaries. The resulting manuscript publications expanded the reach of that research and increased the members' publication productivity. This in turn led to higher visibility of the individuals within the group at their home units and across the university, allowing the individuals to engage with a more diverse group of faculty, further elevating the scholar's profile and providing additional opportunities to expand their mentoring networks (Morton and Gil 2019).

SAY MY NAME, SAY MY NAME: LEVERAGING RELATIONSHIPS FROM MENTORSHIP TO SPONSORSHIP

Sponsorship and mentorship are different activities and result in different outcomes. However, without the advantage of mentorship, the act of sponsorship becomes quite difficult. Sponsorship is the act of backing up or vouching for another person (Griffeth et al. 2021), often in a conversation or opportunity to which the individual being sponsored is not privy. Griffeth et al. (2021) suggest that women are underrepresented in the executive ranks because they are over-mentored, are under-sponsored, and do not receive advocacy from superiors for promotion opportunities. Over-mentoring posits the individual as a limited learner, not ready to work independently or to be a leader.

To counter this narrative, the individual seeking mentorship is encouraged to use confident affirming statements in all their networking interactions. Personal examples of this have occurred for the author on a number of occasions when mentors recognized the skills and abilities exhibited in their personal interactions and then provided the author's name to individuals or groups seeking her expertise. The mentor became her sponsor when they promoted her name in a group she had no previous access to.

Consider the following statement: "I am confident in my ability to organize and execute a research plan from implementation to publication. However, I have difficulty connecting with a data-management team able to execute the quantitative modeling I need to move my research forward." This statement encapsulates the individual's strengths, needs, threats, and opportunities in a few sentences. It is a request for an assist, not a rescue. There is no need to over-mentor this individual; in fact, with just a minor assist, this individual is ready to lead a team. This individual is ready for a sponsor, someone who would speak on their behalf; otherwise, they would be overlooked (Deitte et al. 2019). Self-advocacy and networking are skills that can be developed when an individual understands their needs and the needs of the organization and can describe the path to success.

COMPLETING A PERSONAL SWOT ANALYSIS AND PAYING IT FORWARD

The SWOT analysis is a personal inventory of *strengths* (skills, education, experience, networking, character traits), *weaknesses* (gaps in skill, education, experience, networking, character traits), *opportunities* (technology, economy, geography, trends), and *threats* (gaps in technology, economy, geography, trends, *or* where continued weakness threatens academic productivity). In near-to-peer and peer-to-peer networking, the SWOT analysis can show how each member of the group can provide support to the other. This analysis can be particularly effective in cross-discipline mentorship groups, where qualitative and quantitative researchers work together to move research and publications forward. Further, after working together, the mentor peers have the knowledge, skills, and awareness of each other to promote the others' work. The mentorship has evolved to sponsorship.

Being a test pilot in the academy means relying on the work and goodwill of others to navigate the dynamic tenure and promotion process. Being an engineer is positively engaging with peers and senior faculty while speaking to your own strengths before describing your needs. The institutional barriers faced by Black, minority, and women faculty exist, as does the research on the effective measures to counter them. Individual effort is the one part of the equation you can control. Develop your mentoring network, and the sponsorship will follow.

As a woman faculty of color in the academy and a first-generation college student, the author began her journey as a test pilot. She had no blueprint to follow and relied heavily on the goodwill of others to see her through. But she comes from a long line of "make a way out of no way" people. So when asking politely did not provide her with the desired outcomes, she followed the blueprint she observed in her institution and walked boldly forward, making her own plans. Like a good engineer, she chose her team based on their expertise and ability to communicate effectively with her. Importantly, she set her own meetings, devised a plan she could follow, and used the strengths of her team to execute with the highest level of precision. If she can do it, then you can do it. Start where you are, and don't stop.

REFERENCES

Battle, Dolores E. 1999. "Retention of Minority Faculty in Higher Education." *Perspectives on Issues in Higher Education* 3, no. 2: 7–12.

Benishek, Lois A., Kathleen J. Bieschke, Jeeseon Park, and Suzanne M. Slattery. 2004. "A Multicultural Feminist Model of Mentoring." *Journal of Multicultural Counseling and Development* 32: 428–42.

Cao, Jing, and Yu-Chung Yang. 2013, March. "What Are Mentoring and Sponsoring and How Do They Impact Organizations?" Executive Summaries on Current HR Topics (ILRHR 6640), 1–8. https://ecommons.cornell.edu/bitstream/handle/1813/74471/What_are_mentoring_and_sponsoring_and_how_do_they_impact_organizations.pdf?sequence=1.

Deitte, Lori A., Geraldine B. McGinty, Cheri L. Canon, Reed A. Omary, Pamela T. Johnson, and Priscilla J. Slanetz. 2019. "Shifting from Mentorship to Sponsorship—a Game Changer!" *Journal of the American College of Radiology* 16, no. 4: 498–500.

Edwards, Willie J., and Henry H. Ross. 2018, October. "What Are They Saying? Black Faculty at Predominantly White Institutions of Higher Education." *Journal of Human Behavior in the Social Environment* 28, no. 2: 142–61.

Friberg, Jennifer C., Mandy Frake-Mistak, Ruth Healey, Shannon Sipes, Julie Mooney, Stephanie Sanchez, and Karena Waller. 2021. "A Developmental Framework for Mentorship in SoTL Illustrated by Three Examples of Unseen Opportunities for Mentoring." *Teaching and Learning Inquiry* 9, no. 1: 395–413.

Griffeth, Lauren L., Rubina F. Malik, Solange Charas, and Nekeisha Randall. 2021. "Sponsorship: An Intervention to Accelerate Women's Career Velocity." *The ICFAI Journal of Soft Skills* 15, no. 3: 7–22.

Karam, Eli, Sharon Bowland, N. Rowan, K. Washington, A. R. Perry, C. Collins-Camargo, and A. Archuleta. 2012. "Peer Mentoring among Junior Faculty and Implications for Culture Change." *Professional Development* 15, no. 2: 55–62.

Morton, Benterah C., and Elizabeth Gil. 2019. "Not a Solo Ride: Co-Constructed Peer Mentoring for Early Career Educational Leadership

Faculty." *International Journal of Mentoring and Coaching in Education* 8, no. 4: 361–77.

Willingham-McLain, Laurel, Jason Margolis, and Nicole Klingler. 2019. "Designing and Evaluating a Near-Peer Mentoring Exchange for Early-Career Faculty." *The Journal of Faculty Development* 33, no. 3: 59–70.

CHAPTER 9

The Importance of Developing Effective Mentor-Mentee Relationships in Academia
The Perspectives of Two Women of Color in STEM

Angela D. Broadnax and Verónica A. Segarra

As scholars progress through higher education, identifying mentors and developing mentoring relationships are critical for their career advancement and well-being. This is particularly the case with individuals who belong to groups underrepresented in science, technology, engineering, and math (STEM) fields. Evidence shows that scientists from underrepresented backgrounds in STEM have less access to mentoring resources than scientists from well-represented groups. Access to mentoring resources, in turn, is critical for the development of skills and social capital that is needed for success in academia. For example, when graduate students know how to grow and nurture a network of supportive mentors, the impact of their graduate training is maximized. In the workplace, effective mentorship promotes inclusivity, which fosters career development and advancement.

This chapter discusses the importance of establishing effective mentor-mentee relationships during one's academic training. The authors first briefly explore the scholarly work and perspectives focused on academic mentoring to extract principles and ideas that connect to collective experiences they have witnessed as they have advanced in academia. The authors then share, using pseudonyms as tools, mentoring anecdotes that draw attention to these collective experiences.

THE MENTOR-MENTEE CONTINUUM

Mentoring is generally categorized into two types: instrumental and psychosocial mentoring (Arthur and Kram 1985). In academia, instrumental mentoring provides the mentee with skills and knowledge necessary for success in a given field, while psychosocial mentoring focuses on encouragement and personal support as a mentee learns and survives periods of doubt and failure (Blake-Beard et al. 2011). Both forms of mentoring may be particularly necessary for the development of self-efficacy in underrepresented and women students (Liang et al. 2002; Lent and Brown 2013; Curtin, Malley, and Stewart 2016).

As an individual progresses through the different levels of academic training in their chosen career, their success can be fostered through the establishment of mentoring relationships. Mentoring relationships are traditionally thought to involve a more experienced individual, such as a professor, using their acquired knowledge and experiences to guide the development of a mentee or student into future life and/or career stages (Dahlberg, Byars-Winston, and the National Academies of Sciences, Engineering, and Medicine 2019). Historically, mentor-mentee relationships have been regarded as unidirectional, top-down, and wisdom-conferring alliances (Wright 2015; Dahlberg et al. 2019). However, scholarly work in the area of academic mentoring recognizes that as individuals progress through academia and learn to grow into different roles, they are both mentors and mentees with ever-changing mentoring needs (Wright 2015). This is synergistic with what the authors have experienced throughout their careers in academia.

EFFECTIVE MENTOR-MENTEE RELATIONSHIPS ARE CRITICAL FOR SUCCESS IN ACADEMIC ENVIRONMENTS

Developing Academic Self-Concept and Self-Efficacy

A student's academic self-concept comprises the beliefs, attitudes, and self-perceptions they have about their academic competence and performance (Lent, Brown, and Gore 1997). Academic self-concept serves as an important measure of career commitment (Ulku-Steiner and Kurtz-Costes 2000). Not only do skilled mentors foster students' development in their fields of research, but they also contribute to their developing confidence as practitioners. For example, Curtin, Stewart, and Ostrove (2013) have found that advisor support is associated with a stronger sense of belonging and academic self-concept in doctoral students. Ostrove, Stewart, and Curtin (2011) note that the extent to which students feel they belong in graduate school positively affects their sense of academic self-concept and in turn their commitment to an academic career.

Furthermore, in interviews completed by Bieber and Worley (2006), doctoral students reported that faculty mentors were instrumental in their decision to pursue a career in academia and further helped them to develop as academics. The same is true for undergraduate students; their mentors and scientific advisors can help them develop strong science identities and self-efficacy, which in turn fosters their retention and persistence in science careers (Chemers et al. 2011; Eagan et al. 2013; Graham et al. 2013; Casad, Chang, and Pribbenow 2016; Doer-schuk et al. 2016; Gopalan, Halpin, and Johnson 2018; Ahern-Dodson et al. 2020; Bruthers, Hedman, and Matyas 2021; Campbell-Montalvo et al. 2021; Smith et al. 2021). In fact, negative mentoring experiences can have adverse effects in student development (Limeri et al. 2019).

Sadly, access to mentoring opportunities is not equitably available to all. For example, trainees who identify with backgrounds under-represented in STEM tend to have less access to mentoring than their peers from well-represented groups (Segarra et al. 2021; Dahlberg et al. 2019). Deficits in access to mentoring resources can lead those from underrepresented backgrounds to feel like they do not belong in STEM fields (Seymour and Hewitt 1997; Good, Halpin, and Halpin 2000; Morales et al. 2020).

Developing a Sense of Academic Belonging

From the start of graduate school, doctoral students are tasked with determining if a department or program is a good "fit" for them, asking the question, "Do I belong here?" (Austin 2002; Golde 1998). Relationships established between faculty, staff, and peers play a huge role in the socialization of doctoral students into graduate school (Golde 1998). Lovitts (2001) have found that the difference between doctoral students who completed their PhD programs and those who did not was the degree to which they were integrated into the graduate school community. This is especially true for underrepresented individuals and women, who have reported receiving little mentor support and guidance from faculty advisors (Smith and Davidson 1992; Bruce 1995).

Indeed, the advisor-student relationship is among the most important aspects of a doctoral student's academic career (Zhao, Golde, and McCormick 2007). A good relationship between a doctoral student and his/her advisor has been found to impact both student satisfaction and success in graduate school. Doctoral students view good advisors as those who are supportive and convey a sense of confidence in the doctoral student's ability to succeed (Bell-Ellison and Dedrick 2008). Doctoral students who leave their graduate programs prematurely generally report that their advisors were significantly less interested in them as people, in their research ideas, and in their professional development (Lovitts 2001). Similar dynamics have been found to influence the fit and retention of underrepresented undergraduates in STEM fields (Chemers et al. 2011; Eagan et al. 2013; Graham et al. 2013; Casad et al. 2016; Doerschuk et al. 2016; Gopalan et al. 2018; Ahern-Dodson et al. 2020; Bruthers et al. 2021; Campbell-Montalvo et al. 2021; Smith et al. 2021).

"It Takes a Village": Building and Nurturing a Network of Mentor-Mentee Relationships

As one develops and grows into different roles in academia—from undergraduate to graduate student, from doctoral graduate to post-doctoral trainee, and ultimately to early career faculty member and beyond—one must rely on a multitude of mentors for advice and guidance. Relying on only one mentor is not sufficient. Therefore, one must build and nurture a mentoring network that is made up of individuals with different and complementary talents and strengths. A mentoring network not only should be composed of individuals in more advanced career stages but also should most definitely include peers and near-peers—individuals at similar or comparable career stages.

Moreover, as an individual advances in their academic career and is in a position to share skills or knowledge with others, their mentoring ecosystem will also include those they mentor—their mentees. Mentees are an important part of an individual's mentoring ecosystem, as mentors report gains from engaging in mentoring others, such as improved career preparation and satisfaction, cognitive and socioemotional growth, improved teaching and communication skills, and increased productivity (Dolan and Johnson 2009; Limeri et al. 2019; Diggs-Andrews, Mayer, and Riggs 2021). To build an effective mentoring network, and successfully grow it and nurture it, individuals must be proactive about seeking mentors who will help them fill gaps in their professional development and knowledge (Segarra and Gentry 2021).

LELIA'S STORY

Since her master's degree program, Lelia knew that she wanted to pursue a career as an organic chemistry professor. Despite her career interests, years later, she had chosen to apply to and then join a research program in the biological sciences rather than in organic chemistry. Although not impossible, this route would limit her research opportunities to train as an organic chemist. To exacerbate the situation, Lelia had very little research or coursework experience in the biological sciences. Lelia's primary reason for attending this graduate program was purely because of its reputation both as an elite public university and as a renowned research-intensive program.

However, as a first-generation African American female (a triply underrepresented minority), Lelia felt entirely out of place at this majority-serving institution, a common sentiment of many first-generation underrepresented students (Tate et al. 2015). Not only was she dealing with culture shock, but she was also dealing with feelings of insecurity and doubt as a function of a lack of course training in the biological and biomedical sciences. Had Lelia sought counsel from a mentor such as her master's degree advisor, she might have come to the conclusion that despite the university's reputation as a major research institution, the graduate program itself was not the best fit considering her career aspirations.

Despite Lelia's lack of training in this area, her unrelenting persistence compelled her to push through in pursuit of a doctoral degree even if it was in the wrong field of study per se. To that end, Lelia had a plan to merge the two disciplines and join a lab that would allow her to complete research focusing on the synthesis of organic molecules for biological application(s). At the time, there were fewer than a handful of labs that did the type of work that aligned with her research interests. After much deliberation, Lelia reached out to Carl, the man who would become her research advisor over the next two years.

When Lelia joined the lab, she was suffering from low academic self-concept and self-efficacy as it related to her future in graduate school and in her academic career. And joining a lab with eleven graduate students and one post-doc didn't help to add to her sense of self. In a relatively large lab, it wasn't impossible to speak with her research advisor, but as one might expect, initially Lelia was trained by a senior graduate student. The only issue with this is that a senior graduate student is largely focused on wrapping up their thesis project in time for their defense date. Lelia was able to glean as much information as possible, but when her peer mentor left, it was on her to develop a viable research project.

The project Lelia proposed was central to the lab's research focus, but it involved a large amount of organic synthesis of molecules. Lelia was left to figure it out on her own with the exception of receiving some support from students in her lab and a post-doctoral fellow in another research lab. However, the contributions from her peers were not enough, especially since she did not have a strong research background in the area. Because her research advisor did not have academic training in organic chemistry, he could not offer much instrumental mentorship. Furthermore, Carl's style of mentoring was more of a "sink or swim" approach, so Lelia—along with the others of her lab— was left to learn how to figure it out on her own or risk drowning.

The lab environment was not the right fit for Lelia, as it was not a place she was thriving in due to intense pressure both from herself and from her research advisor. After failed attempts at her proposed project coupled with a lack of psychosocial support from her advisor, Lelia sought advice from two female professors who served on her graduate school committee. They confirmed what she felt she should do—leave her lab due to a lack of instrumental and psychosocial support. Lelia needed to leave not just the lab but also the program as well due to her lack of interest in studying biological and biomedical sciences. She left the program having obtained a master's degree in biological sciences.

Despite this setback, Lelia did not give up on her dreams of receiving a doctoral degree in organic chemistry and becoming an organic chemistry professor. She applied to and was accepted into a chemistry graduate program, where she studied organic chemistry. After five years of graduate school training, Lelia completed her dissertation and earned her doctorate.

ADELA'S STORY

Adela began her undergraduate scientific training at a large public university located in a U.S. territory. Adela's mother tongue was Spanish, with a little bit of Spanglish (Nash 2015) mixed in—she grew up drinking *café con leche* in the mornings, learned how to drive in her grandmother's *carro*, and loved to *janguear* with her sisters and cousins. When it was time to apply for college, she knew she wanted to be a scientist. She ultimately chose a discipline that fell somewhere between biology and chemistry—biochemistry.

She did really well in her first year of college but encountered difficulty as a rising sophomore gaining access to the courses she needed to advance in her program because of long course waiting lists and slow course periodicities. Access to mentors and faculty members with the time to help with advice was also lacking. This drove her to make a decision she had not even considered before—to leave her homeland and transfer to a university in the United States. Had Adela been able to access a reliable mentoring network, she may have been able to find solutions to the challenges she encountered as a rising sophomore, potentially allowing her to stay in her homeland and contribute to its STEM talent.

Sophomore year in the United States was a struggle for Adela—transitioning from being an occasional academic user of English for specific courses to a full-time English user for practical and academic purposes. Adela became self-conscious about her accent to the point that the only way to move forward was to stop caring about what others thought about her English abilities. Once the yoke was lifted, her newly found freedom allowed her to work on becoming comfortable as a scholar. Adela started visiting the university's writing center every week to perfect her English writing skills, and she looked for opportunities to engage in research and in laboratory-based advanced STEM courses—in these experiences, she found her love for science again and started developing a vision for the future. She also found peers, professors, and senior researchers who helped her sculpt a plan to realize her goal of becoming an independent scientist. These individuals became a reliable network of mentors who would serve as a sounding board whenever challenges would arise. When Adela was deciding which graduate school programs to apply to, one of her scientific advisors encouraged her to aim higher. She ultimately earned admission into a graduate program that once had seemed "out-of-reach."

The time came for Adela to move to attend graduate school, way up north, where winter was full of snow and down coats. Independence as a scientist was expected and had to be developed in flight. Once these experiences were way in the past, Adela later realized that she had always had at least one mentor, many times a peer or near-peer, who was willing to help her as best as they could. In fact, she had relied on her network of mentors for help, even though they were not geographically in close proximity. Adela's network of mentors had helped her sustain her effort and resilience during graduate school. Almost two decades after having ultimately earned her doctorate degree, she identifies with the poem "Accents" by Denice Frohman (2013):

Her accent is a stubborn compass
Always pointing her
Towards home.

Adela's only regret is not having built her mentoring network earlier in her career. Had she done that, she may have been able to become a scientist in her homeland.

THE IMPORTANCE OF DEVELOPING EFFECTIVE MENTOR-MENTEE RELATIONSHIPS IN ACADEMIA

There is ultimately no one prescriptive way to successfully build, expand, and nurture a mentoring network. Each individual can decide how to build and maintain their network in ways that are consistent with their values and perceptions of success. Sometimes mentoring relationships can be hard to navigate since they are built on interpersonal dynamics and interactions. As long as one brings patience, grace, empathy, honesty, and the desire to do right by ourselves and the members of our network to these interactions, one will hit the ground running toward success.

REFERENCES

Ahern-Dodson, J., C. R. Clark, T. Mourad, and J. A. Reynolds. 2020. "Beyond the Numbers: Understanding How a Diversity Mentoring Program Welcomes Students into a Scientific Community." *Ecosphere* 11, no. 2.

Arthur, Michael B., and Kathy E. Kram. 1985. "Mentoring at Work: Developmental Relationships in Organizational Life." *Administrative Science Quarterly* 30, no. 3: 454–54.

Austin, Ann E. 2002. "Preparing the Next Generation of Faculty: Graduate School as Socialization to the Academic Career." *The Journal of Higher Education* 73, no. 1: 94–122.

Bell-Ellison, Bethany A., and Robert F Dedrick. 2008. "What Do Doctoral Students Value in Their Ideal Mentor?" *Research in Higher Education* 49, no. 6.

Bieber, Jeffery P., and Linda K. Worley. 2006. "Conceptualizing the Academic Life: Graduate Students' Perspectives." *The Journal of Higher Education* 77, no. 6: 1009–35.

Blake-Beard, Stacy, Melissa L. Bayne, Faye J. Crosby, and Carol B. Muller. 2011. "Matching by Race and Gender in Mentoring Relationships: Keeping Our Eyes on the Prize." *The Journal of Social Issues* 67, no. 3: 622–43.

Bruce, M. A. 1995. "Mentoring Women Doctoral Students: What Counselor Educators and Supervisors Can Do." *Counselor Education and Supervision* 35, no. 2: 139–49.

Bruthers, C. B., E. L. Hedman, and M. L. Matyas. 2021. "Undergraduate Research Programs Build Skills for Diverse Students." *Advances in Physiology Education* 45, no. 2: 399–408.

Campbell-Montalvo, Rebecca, Gladis Kersaint, Chrystal A. S. Smith, Ellen Puccia, John Skvoretz, Hesborn Wao, Julie P. Martin, George MacDonald, and Reginald Lee. 2021. "How Stereotypes and Relationships Influence Women and Underrepresented Minority Students' Fit in Engineering." *Journal of Research in Science Teaching* 59, no. 4: 656–92.

Casad, Bettina J., A. L. Chang, and C. M. Pribbenow. 2016. "The Benefits of Attending the Annual Biomedical Research Conferences for Minority Students (ABRCMS): The Role of Research Confidence." *CBE—Life Sciences Education* 15, no. 3.

Chemers, M. M., E. L. Zurbriggen, M. Syed, B. K. Goza, and S. Bearman. 2011. "The Role of Efficacy and Identity in Science Career Commitment among Underrepresented Minority Students." *Journal of Social Issues* 67, no. 3: 469–91.

Curtin, Nicola, Abigail J. Stewart, and Joan M. Ostrove. 2013. "Fostering Academic Self-Concept: Advisor Support and Sense of Belonging among International and Domestic Graduate Students." *American Educational Research Journal* 50, no. 1: 108–37.

Curtin, Nicola, Janet Malley, and Abigail J. Stewart. 2016. "Mentoring the Next Generation of Faculty: Supporting Academic Career Aspirations among Doctoral Students." *Research in Higher Education* 57, no. 6: 714–38.

Dahlberg, Maria Lund, Angela Byars-Winston, and the National Academies of Sciences, Engineering, and Medicine. 2019. *The Science of Effective Mentorship in STEMM*. Washington, DC: National Academies Press.

Diggs-Andrews, K. A., D. G. Mayer, and B. Riggs. 2021, June. "Introduction to Effective Mentorship for Early-Career Research Scientists." *BMC Proceedings* 15, no. 2: 1–7.

Doerschuk, P., C. Bahrim, J. Daniel, J. Kruger, J. Mann, and C. Martin. 2016. "Closing the Gaps and Filling the STEM Pipeline: A Multidisciplinary Approach." *Journal of Science Education and Technology* 25, no. 4: 682–95.

Dolan, E., and D. Johnson. 2009. "Toward a Holistic View of Undergraduate Research Experiences: An Exploratory Study of Impact on Graduate/Postdoctoral Mentors." *Journal of Science Education and Technology* 18, no. 6: 487–500.

Eagan Jr., M. K., S. Hurtado, M. J. Chang, G. A. Garcia, F. A. Herrera, and J. C. Garibay. 2013. "Making a Difference in Science Education: The Impact of Undergraduate Research Programs." *American Educational Research Journal* 50, no. 4: 683–713.

Frohman, Denice. 2013. "Accents." Available online at https://narrativenorth east.com/?p=1952.

Golde, Chris M. 1998. "Beginning Graduate School: Explaining First-Year Doctoral Attrition." *New Directions for Higher Education* 1998: 55–64.

Good, J. M., G. Halpin, and G. Halpin. 2000. "A Promising Prospect for Minority Retention: Students Becoming Peer Mentors." *Journal of Negro Education* 69, no. 4: 375–83.

Gopalan, C., P. A. Halpin, and K. M. Johnson. 2018. "Benefits and Logistics of Nonpresenting Undergraduate Students Attending a Professional Scientific Meeting." *Advances in Physiology Education* 42, no. 1: 68–74.

Graham, M. J., J. Frederick, A. Byars-Winston, A. B. Hunter, and J. Handelsman. 2013. "Increasing Persistence of College Students in STEM." *Science* 341, no. 6153: 1455–56.

Lent, Robert W., and Steven D. Brown. 2013. "Social Cognitive Model of Career Self-Management: Toward a Unifying View of Adaptive Career Behavior Across the Life Span." *Journal of Counseling Psychology* 60, no. 4: 557–68.

Lent, Robert W., Steven D. Brown, and Paul A. Gore. 1997. "Discriminant and Predictive Validity of Academic Self-Concept, Academic Self-Efficacy, and Mathematics-Specific Self-Efficacy." *Journal of Counseling Psychology* 44, no. 3: 307–15.

Liang, Belle, Allison J. Tracy, Catherine A. Taylor, and Linda M. Williams. 2002. "Mentoring College-Age Women: A Relational Approach." *American Journal of Community Psychology* 30, no. 2: 271–88.

Limeri, Lisa B., Muhammad Zaka Asif, Benjamin H. T. Bridges, David Esparza, Trevor T. Tuma, Daquan Sanders, Alexander J. Morrison, Pallavi Rao, Joseph A. Harsh, Adam V. Maltese, Erin L. Dolan, and Joel K. Abraham. 2019. "'Where's My Mentor?!' Characterizing Negative Mentoring Experiences in Undergraduate Life Science Research." *CBE—Life Sciences Education* 18, no. 4: ar61.

Lovitts, B. E. 2001. *Leaving the Ivory Tower: The Causes and Consequences of Departure from Doctoral Study.* Lanham, MD: Rowman & Littlefield.

Morales N., K. Bisbee O'Connell, S. McNulty, A. Berkowitz, G. Bowser, M. Giamellaro, and M. N. Miriti. 2020. "Promoting Inclusion in Ecological Field Experiences: Examining and Overcoming Barriers to a Professional Rite of Passage." *The Bulletin of the Ecological Society of America* 101, no. 4.

Nash, R. 2015. "Spanglish: Language Contact in Puerto Rico." In *Perspectives on American English*, edited by Joey L. Dillard, 265–76. Berlin; Boston: De Gruyter Mouton.

Ostrove, J. M., A. J. Stewart, and N. L. Curtin. 2011. "Social Class and Belonging: Implications for Graduate Students' Career Aspirations." *Journal of Higher Education* 82, no. 6.

Segarra, V. A., and W. A. Gentry. 2021, June. "Taking Ownership of Your Career: Professional Development through Experiential Learning." *BMC Proceedings* 15, no. 2: 1–7.

Segarra, V. A., J. Vigoreaux, M. E. Zavala, and A. Edwards. 2021, June. "Accomplishing Career Transitions 2019: Facilitating Success towards the Professoriate." *BMC Proceedings* 15, no. 2: 1–2.

Seymour, E., and N. M. Hewitt. 1997. *Talking about Leaving*. Boulder, CO: Westview Press.

Smith, Chrystal A. S., Hesborn Wao, Gladis Kersaint, Rebecca Campbell-Montalvo, Phyllis Gray-Ray, Ellen Puccia, Julie P. Martin, Reginald Lee, John Skvoretz, and George MacDonald. 2021. "Social Capital from Professional Engineering Organization and Persistence of Women and Underrepresented Minority Undergraduates." *Frontiers in Sociology* 6.

Smith, E. P., and W. S. Davidson. 1992. "Mentoring and the Development of African-American Graduate Students." *Journal of College Student Development* 33, no. 6: 531–39.

Tate, K. A., W. Caperton, D. Kaiser, N. T. Pruitt, H. White, and E. Hall. 2015. "An Exploration of First-Generation College Students' Career Development Beliefs and Experiences." *Journal of Career Development* 42, no. 4: 294–310.

Ulku-Steiner, Beril, and Beth Kurtz-Costes. 2000. "Doctoral Student Experiences in Gender-Balanced and Male-Dominated Graduate Programs." *Journal of Educational Psychology* 92, no. 2: 296–307.

Wright, Glenn, ed. 2015. *The Mentoring Continuum: From Graduate School through Tenure*. Syracuse, NY: Graduate School Press of Syracuse University.

Zhao, Chun-Mei, Chris M. Golde, and Alexander C. McCormick. 2007. "More Than a Signature: How Advisor Choice and Advisor Behaviour Affect Doctoral Student Satisfaction." *Journal of Further and Higher Education* 31, no. 3: 263–81.

CHAPTER 10

Bringing in Afrocentric Values to Mentor African American Students

Annie Ruth Leslie

Since at least as early as when Black Contraband soldiers fought along-side Union soldiers in the American Civil War because they wanted an education, the importance of getting an education cannot be overstated. The Contraband soldiers fought valiantly because they wanted to get an education, attain economic security, and be able to vote—in that order. Since the American Civil War up through Jim Crow and today, scholars acknowledge that the educational sojourn of Black Americans has been an uphill struggle.

For example, Jarvis Givens (2021) chronicles these struggles in his book *Fugitive Pedagogy*, in which he writes that during the late nineteenth and early twentieth centuries, the Black American scholar and teacher Carter G. Woodson and other contemporary dedicated Black teachers forged what Givens called a *fugitive* educational pedagogy to advance the study of Black history and learning in southern and northern Black schools. The fugitive pedagogy exists to minimize the legal and institutional racism that stymies Black education. Givens writes that this fugitive or underground way of teaching "reveals the heritage of black education to be a plot of perpetual escape, always striving toward a world where what is known to be human is not premised on the subjection of black life" (p. 25).

Bettina Love (2019), another young Black scholar, discusses the uphill educational struggles of Black Americans in her book *We Want to Do More Than Survive*. Love advises educators to scrap individual grade-point-average (GPA) and test-taking models that feed a profit-making orientation and, instead, engage in abolitionist teaching that allows students to understand the intersectional nature of Black educational marginalization and racist, classist, sexist, and homophobic systems of oppression. Love argues that once this is fully understood and embraced, Black teaching will become a liberatory endeavor.

What follows in this chapter is s brief discussion of theoretical perspectives that examine Black students' academic challenges to then compare these to the author's and other scholars' personal reflections about their education and mentoring during their early educational sojourn.

THEORETICAL PERSPECTIVES: AFRICAN AMERICAN STUDENT DEVELOPMENT

While Givens and Love are critical of deficit models that focus on individual deficiencies, there exists in sociology, for instance, a mixed approach to understanding the educational challenges Black students confront. For example, some interaction theories (IT) include a "fix the individual" approach to Black Americans' low GPAs and graduation rates (Williams, Coles, and Reynolds 2020). IT is based on the idea that individuals define their own situation through interactions with others where they give meaning to themselves and to others. IT provides insights into the impact on self of the ways, for instance, Whites marginalize Blacks. In education, for example, interactionists observe how things such as a teacher's low expectation of Black students can negatively affect students' academic performance (Barkan 2017; Cuyjet 2006).

Critical race theory (CRT) veers away from individual actions/reactions/inactions to examine social structural factors as impediments to Black educational development. When CRT scholars examine, for instance, the impact of affirmative action policies (integration of schools by race quotas) on Black students, schools, and communities, they conclude that attempts to establish racial equality by busing Black children out of their communities to far-away White schools are not ideal because integration is not a substitute for quality learning and that having a Black child bused to a White school guaranteed that millions and millions of state and national dollars and other resources would flow to the White schools where Black children are bused, leaving

Black schools that serve the larger Black community worse off than before affirmative action (Crenshaw 1991; Crenshaw et al. 1995; Cho, Crenshaw, and McCall 2013; Nichols and Stahl 2019; Givens 2021; Love 2019). Similarly to CRT, another group of social scientists refers to White supremacy as the "invisible hand" on the scale tipping it toward White supremacy and away from Black student success (Leslie et al. 2021).

Another perspective, culturally relevant care (CRC) mentoring, proposes that Black student success is related to a mentoring that brings in the students' own cultural values. That is, the way to get Black students to participate in their own education is to make education relevant to them (Reddick and Pritchett 2016; Sealey-Ruiz and Greene 2011). At the same time, they acknowledge that mentoring Black students can be complicated by such things as mentor bias or ethnocentrism. Moreover, one weakness in CRC is the failure to identify the principles that guide selection of Black cultural values. These researchers caution that more research needs to be done in this area (Reddick and Pritchett 2016; Sealey-Ruiz and Greene 2011).

There is a resemblance between culturally relevant care and Afrocentric (ACT) perspectives—both are concerned with the cultural values of African Americans. One, however, is concerned with the use of Black values to mentor students (CRC) and the other to teach, develop school curricula, and mentor (ACT).

Afrocentric generally refers to a frame of reference from which social phenomena is viewed from the perspective of the African person (Asante 1991). Molefe Asante recognizes that Black people's absence from Eurocentric scholarship is harmful to Black students, and he writes about this harm in much the same way as did Carter G. Woodson.

Asante writes:

In most classrooms, whatever the subject, whites are located in the center perspective position. How alien the African American child must feel, how like an outsider! The little African American child who sits in a classroom and is taught to accept as heroes and heroines individuals who defamed African people is actively being de-centered, dislocated and made into a nonperson.

Asante also writes that when African American students can see themselves as subjects rather than as objects of education, be it "discipline, biology, medicine, literature, or social studies," Black students can become recentered, thus preparing them to be active participants in their own education.

Asante's observation about the cultural centering of oneself in one's Africanity can be a complicated issue, as scholar Gomez (1998) reminds us when he describes the linguistic, economic, and class struggles that transpired in the making of a unique African American culture among enslaved Niger/Congolese Africans. Bettina Love (2019), however, provides an interesting concept of *joy* to center oneself in abolitionist teaching and mentoring. She observes that to know an enslaved or marginalized group's joy can be liberating in that knowledge of this joy allows one to take that joy and utilize it to resist oppression. This is to say, if the enslaved ancestors' joy derived from singing Negro spirituals, then others can sing these songs, allowing the joy felt by the ancestors to become one's own joy—a joy that one can use as a weapon to teach resistance. What follows are some personal reflections of Black scholars and the joys that shaped their lives and allowed them to achieve academic success.

PERSONAL REFLECTIONS: BLACK HISTORY WEEK

In Moorhead, the small Mississippi Delta cotton town where the author attended a segregated Moorhead Coloured Elementary School, there were outside toilets called *outhouses* with no running water or sanitation. The author loved basketball and never thought twice about having to play on an outside dirt basketball court. The school's edifice was very similar to those where Carter G. Woodson worked during the late nineteenth and early twentieth centuries. In Moorhead, as elsewhere in Mississippi, schools for White children were well equipped with indoor bathrooms and running water, inside swimming pools, and gyms, the latest textbooks, and libraries. Black teachers taught Black students the basics from long-outdated books inherited from the White Moorhead Elementary School—the White school's name was stamped on the inside cover of the donated books.

In spite of very limited material resources, they had dedicated Black teachers who did more than their best with the few resources they had. It was these teachers who organized a Black History Week (as it was called then) every February, which was actually a commemoration of ancestors such as George Washington Carver, Phyllis Wheatley, Booker T. Washington, Mary McLeod Bethune, Ida B. Wells, Fredrick Douglass, and others. Hungry for this rare Black commemorative event, Black students attended Black history activities with pompous and renewed interest in learning. This week of indulgence in the culture of Black heroes and sheroes was water for the thirsty—creating in the author an insatiable hunger and thirst for knowledge about Black people. She liked the warm feeling and the rush she felt when running ahead into the classroom where everyone assembled—it was better than church because they didn't see this as boring, but an exciting event.

Black History Week provided a special time for educational learning because the standard school curriculum included racist books with stories about characters such as Little Black Sambo, an African child who ran so fast pulling a tiger's tail that he turned into butter. Africa was presented primarily as the home to Tarzan, a White man living in Africa swinging from tree to tree, but who was considered lord of the jungle, reigning over awe-stricken and scantily dressed Africans. These were prevalent presentations of Africans, and even today—in spite of books such as *Black Athena* (Bernal 1987), which carefully details the Black presence in pre- and dynastic Egypt—there remains many questions about the important role of Blacks in Egypt other than as slaves. For instance, there are those who write that the Sphinx was White and that the Black Egyptian mummies housed in English and German museum basements are Black only because their White skin darkened over the years. And even some Black scientists who study Black family experiences—such as unwed motherhood (Frazuier 1941) or the crack epidemic, for example—see these as personal, not structural, problems.

In a recent documentary, the legendary Civil Rights activist Fannie Lou Hamer (Davenport 2022), spoke with pride about her first trip to Ghana, West Africa, where she saw Black people at the helm of their banks, stores, businesses, and institutions—inspiring her to continue struggling for human rights in Mississippi.

Notably, it was the yearly February Black History Weeks in Moorhead that inspired the author to believe she could compete successfully, not only against Whites in the state and national spelling bees but also to become a Phyllis Wheatley or Queen of Sheba or other commemorated Black ancestor. This feeling of being special continued into the author's membership in a Black secret society.

MENTORSHIP IN A "SECRET SOCIETY"

The author will not soon forget the joy of a community mother/elder, Ms. Lula Garner, who lived in Moorhead. Mrs. Garner was a slightly heavyset woman with White hair washed over with a light bluish rinse (worn fashionably by some older Black women). She was a Black woman who looked White, had a quiet, dignified way of smiling and speaking, and loved the Black community. She belonged to the middle-class Mount Ararat Baptist Church in Moorhead, whereas the author's family belonged to the working-class Second Baptist Pleasant Green Church. Pleasant Green had the best preacher, though, and even some of the Mount Ararat crowd found themselves at Pleasant Green every fourth Sunday on Pastoral Day when the preacher delivered his sermon from the pulpit.

Reverend Mayes was not college-trained like Reverend Matthew, the pastor at Mount Ararat Church, but everyone said he could really preach. That is, he didn't just read from the Bible and talk his sermon (as did Reverend Matthews of Mount Ararat), but he would read from the Bible first and then put the book down, and between start and finish, he admonished members about good behavior, told jokes, shouted, screamed, screeched, laughed, made those gasping sounds in his throat that only good preachers could—he would make these sound nearing the end of every sentence until he opened up the church for members wanting to join. During these heady times, church mothers would *shout* before the sermon ended. Church mothers shouted in our church because they "felt the spirit." However, these shout patterns did not occur in the Mount Ararat Church.

Church mothers shouted differently, with some throwing their heads back while stretching out both arms, and some made mourning-like sounds with their eyes closed as if they couldn't breathe while others walked about shouting "hallelujah" and "thank you, Jesus." When church mothers shouted, church ushers would quickly run to their side to fan and comfort them. Once in a while, the author would see Mrs. Lula Garner at the church, but what the author found dear about her was that Mrs. Garner recruited her into a secret society that Mrs. Garner led.

They had many secrets that they were never to share with others. Even the author's mother didn't know the secret password needed for all their meetings and social gatherings. Their secret society group consisted of five young girls aged 13–15 who would meet at Mrs. Garner's home, but sometimes they traveled with her to Rulesville, Mississippi, another nearby town with a chapter of their secret society. They had to recite the secret password before they could enter her home. Rulesville was also home to Mrs. Fannie Lou Hamer, the noted Black civil rights leader.

Mrs. Garner was what scholar Patricia Hill Collins (1991) calls a "community mother." She had no children of her own, but she was dedicated to teaching those young girls, and this gave the author a feeling of being special. She instilled in them information about their ancestors and their history. She treated them with love and care—they were the children she hoped would elevate the race. She continually reminded them that they were the flowers of their race and that they could do and be whatever they worked to be, if they worked hard at it.

As young members of their society, they were groomed to participate in a speech competition wherein winners received a scholarship for college. The author didn't win the competition, but she always knew where she wanted to go to college— Mississippi Vocational College (MVC). During her adolescence, her father took her and her six siblings to the neighboring town of Itta Bena, Mississippi, where a new HBCU was being built by the state: Mississippi Vocational College. That trip was one of the few times her father's pride rivaled the pride she saw when he would tell them Br'er Rabbit stories, where the hero rabbit made use of clever but complicated tricks to win the day.

Mrs. Garner was also a community mother who brought to their town the *National Chicago Defender*—the only Black national newspaper in Chicago. Mrs. Garner had contacts in Chicago, and she distributed

Defender papers to all in Moorhead. The paper gave Moorhead Black residents a glimpse into the outside political world. It's unlikely the White residents of Moorhead even knew that Mrs. Garner distributed the newspaper to Black residents, but the paper did allow Black adults and elders to stay abreast of national news.

The *Chicago Defender* was a Black-owned newspaper that gave the news from a Black perspective. Mrs. Garner had dozens of copies sent to her weekly, and she in turn gave them to Black people who wanted to know something about Black news, politics, and social life. It was through this newspaper that the author came to read about the "evil eye," an Egyptian icon associated with secret knowledge. Another notable part of the Black world the author learned about during her youth was the spirituals—the sorrow songs of her enslaved ancestors.

THE SPIRITUALS: MENTORSHIP VIA
THE ANCESTORS' ENERGY FORCE

If *mentoring* refers to the knowledge an elder or faculty passes on to the young, then another mentor the author had was Mrs. Julia Mae Taylor, her eighth-grade teacher, who taught her the words of the spirituals. Spirituals are the so-called sorrow songs enslaved African sang in the cotton fields. They sang about loneliness for their homes in Africa and from their families and communal life they left behind. For the author's eighth-grade graduation ceremony, Mrs. Taylor taught them to sing spirituals. They practiced many days and hours for this ceremony, and Mrs. Taylor, who played the piano, taught them the lyrics of about six or so spirituals, including "I Couldn't Hear Nobody Pray" and "Deep River." One such song spoke of the ancestors' alienation: "I was way down yonder all by myself and I couldn't hear nobody pray—oh my Lawdee, I couldn't hear nobody pray." Another one was "Deep river, my home is over Jordan. Deep river, I want to cross over into campground." Most writers agree that the home mentioned in the spirituals was Africa, the home they were forced to leave behind.

Mrs. Taylor was the kind of teacher who writer Bettina Love (2019) called an abolitionist teacher. Mrs. Taylor expected excellence and taught the author about the importance of Black history and being dignified. At the time, the author had heard about the spirituals during

Black History Week but had not heard or sang them. The author doesn't know exactly what gave their enslaved ancestors the strength they exhibited under such harsh conditions of enslavement, but Eugene Genovese (1972), Herskovits (1941), and Sterling Stuckey (1987) write that it was their Niger/Congolese life-affirming belief in a benevolent God force that would eventually prevail—these sorrow songs became the joys of the enslaved who sang these songs together, but sometimes alone.

Stuckey (1987) writes that the enslaved shared in a ring shout they performed at religious activities. They sang these songs to give themselves hope and spiritual healing. Faulkner (1978) writes that it was in their Br'er Rabbit storytelling that they could see themselves as that clever rabbit who would always win in his various exploits—he won because he was smart and used his head for more than a hat rack. Rabbit was their clever hero who used his intellectual, not physical, prowess to win whenever he came up against predators. The author didn't learn about the didactic nature of Rabbit's exploits until much later in life, but at the time, she remembers how animated and happy her father would be when telling them those stories. The enslaved identified with the hero rabbit—he was their hero—their joy.

It would be years later in the author's adulthood that she would be inspired by historian Sterling Stuckey to write papers about Br'er Rabbit's meaning in Black culture.

WHITE FACULTY MENTORSHIP OF AFRICAN AMERICAN SCHOLARS

A noted African American mathematician and scholar, Joshua Leslie graduated from the La Sorbonne in Paris with a PhD in mathematics during the late 1960s. He attributed his academic achievements to his White teacher mentor at the all-Black DuSable High School in Chicago, Illinois. The faculty mentor, a single woman who chose to work at a Black high school, provided mentoring resembling what today is called culturally relevant care. Leslie recalls how Ms. Herrick shaped his future academic development and scholarship by her willingness to give her full care to support him and one other Black student attending DuSable High School: Sterling Stuckey, who went on to write the award-winning book *Slave Culture*, was equally shaped by Ms. Herrick's caring mentorship.

Both Leslie and Stuckey loved Ms. Herrick and thought that she was a living example of one who lived what she taught. She believed in her Black students' academic abilities and actively encouraged them to reach high—an encouragement that was especially important after another White counselor had advised Leslie to aim high by becoming a mechanic. About Ms. Herrick, Leslie notes: "She gave me a sense of genuine concern for my wellbeing and intellectual development and she appreciated that my intellectual development and concerns for wellbeing were the same."

Leslie observes how Ms. Herrick embraced another Black high school student, Sterling Stuckey, who also characterized her mentorship as genuine concern for her students that translated into her encouraging her civics (American government) class students to read the great books, go to college, and recognize their own heritage and genius. At the time of these civics classes, Chicago was one of the most segregated, racist, and violent communities in the United States, home to one of the worst race riots in the twentieth century.

Despite the racist and sexist times during which Leslie, Stuckey, and others lived in Chicago, other great African American scholars—such as Carter G. Woodson—had great mentors like Ms. Herrick. It was actually Woodson's two uncles who mentored and taught him the importance of doing research about African and African American history (Bell 1992).

MENTORING UNDERGRADUATE BLACK STUDENTS IN RESEARCH

As an adult, it was actually sitting with Joshua Leslie and Sterling Stuckey night after night after night over a period of year listening to them talk about what would later become *Slave Culture* that the author became interested in mentoring two undergraduate students at her university. Stuckey and Leslie were a great team: Sterling would write passionately to capture Leslie's words. Sterling had a way with words that Leslie loved, and so as Leslie talked, Sterling would write. It was Leslie who lived in Nigeria for almost ten years and had an intimate knowledge of Niger/Congolese cultures. These men peaked the author's interest in later mentoring two students at her university as they had been mentored in their youth.

Teaching at Bowie State University allowed the author to take underwing two students who became a part of a faculty-student research institute funded by the National Science Foundation: the Semester-based Undergraduate Research Institute (SURI). The research program connects students with faculty members' research. There, faculty researchers take on undergraduate students and train them to be involved in the faculty's research, a project where the student, as a junior member of the team, is mentored and taught how to conduct research by actually doing it.

During the spring and summer semesters of 2021, the author and another colleague mentored two African American undergraduate students in the SURI Program, where undergraduate mentees acquaint themselves with faculty research. In this case, the research involved the study of police violence against African American males—a topic dear to many in the Black community, especially after the police murder of George Floyd, an African American male whose murder was videotaped and watched by the world.

SURI mentees do not have low academic GPAs but have limited research skills that mentors work to develop. The author and colleague were able to successfully train their mentees by capturing their interest with a vivid portrayal of race relations in America (aka critical race theory). Similar to critical race theory—where the intersectional nature of a profit-making system of legal slave codes is related to the privatization of prisons and the violence of White officers who oversee the maintenance of this system—the mentees began to understand these connections. That is, the student mentees came to understand the intersectionality of police brutality and our profit-oriented capitalist system of racism, sexism, sharecropping, slave and penal codes, and Supreme Court decisions.

As the mentees read books about race and culture, they became more interested, asked cogent questions, and offered very good suggestions about changes needed in their focus group methodology. After six months of readings, forums, and study, both mentees were able to facilitate four focus groups and critically develop themes emanating from these—all notable academic accomplishments. Finally, because the faculty mentors sympathized with their mentees' interest in racial justice, and acquainted them with books about African and African American culture, the mentees' interest in Black male incarceration increased their fervor for teaching social work with the passion of what scholar Bettina Love (2019) calls "abolition teaching." It also led to them making serious contributions to the publication of an article (Leslie et al. forthcoming). Presently, they both conduct graduate research at two notable universities in Maryland and Washington, DC.

DISCUSSION

In this chapter, the author presents primarily personal reflections about mentoring that she, along with other scholars, received during childhood and adolescence. Theoretical perspectives about Black student educational success and mentoring are also presented to situate what has been discussed about Black student academic challenges and successes. The author refers to these personal reflections as Afrocentric joys, including the author's joy associated with Black History Weeks and learning about Black institutions and the experiences of her ancestors; joy emanating from being mentored by community mothers and family; joy in belonging to a secret society; joy in learning to sing the spirituals; joy in mentoring undergraduates; and lastly, joy in knowing that someone else's community mothering mattered.

Herein, a composite profile emerges where the joys exemplify an ethos that Bettina Love (2019) would call a "joy and hope" ethos. That is, joy by another name is hope, and hope survives slavery, sorrow, injustice, and oppression. Joy and hope are, therefore, the starting points for an Afrocentric education and mentoring, where the joys teach children how to not merely survive but to thrive and excel.

The author has long been impressed by enslaved Africans who found it possible to direct themselves—they were able to inspire themselves by looking at their cultural past as the children of Africa. Their oppressors were not able to make them have real contempt for themselves as a people. Rather, they had contempt (sometimes pity) for those who oppressed and forced on them an animal existence. Their oppressors were not able to thwart their *spirit of freedom* or their *knowledge of their dignity*. Yes, some threw themselves overboard the slave ships bringing them to the New World, but even those forced to lie in their own excrement on those ships knew this was not something of their nature or cultural traditions.

It was natural for enslaved community fathers like Denmark Vesey and Nat Turner to revolt, including those White community fathers like John Brown and his sons—they were not cowed. Even with the inhuman treatment many experienced during slavery and after, African Americans prayed, sang the spirituals, told folk stories of their past, raised their families, and passed on to children their values about life, death, and how to survive—thereby living to see another day until their joys and hopes reached present-day generations of teachers who were energized by these joys and hopes coming from the ancestors.

What explains New World Africans' cultural sense of freedom, dignity, and the will to live? Herein lies an Afrocentric field of study to begin to educate and mentor our children. That is, scholars are responsible for doing the scholarly work of studying African American joys and hopes as these teach those in all relevant disciplines to understand not only the past but also how this past shapes African people's spirit of freedom, knowledge of dignity, and sense of themselves as children of the African cultural tradition. Herein lies a historical and sociocultural framework for the development of a curriculum of courses aimed at the discovery of the ontological meaning of these African American and Niger/Congolese life-affirming values. Moreover, herein is a viable framework for African American students to be immersed in an educational curriculum and mentorship that examines these themes of joy and hope to make students an integral part of and active participants in their education.

REFERENCES

Asante, Molefe. 1991. "The Afrocentric Idea in Education." *The Journal of Negro Education* 60, no. 2: 170.

Barkan, Steve. 2017. *Sociology: Understanding and Changing the Social World.* Boston, MA: FlatWorld Publishers.

Bell, Derrick. 1992. *Faces at the Bottom of the Well.* New York: Basic Books.

Bernal, Martin. 1987. *Black Athena*. London: Free Association Press.

Cho, S., K. Crenshaw, and L. McCall. 2013. "Toward a Field of Intersectionality Studies: Theory, Application, and Praxis." *Signs* (Chicago, IL) 38, no. 4: 787–810.

Crenshaw, K. 2019. "Mapping the Margins: Intersectionality, Identity Politics, and Violence against Women of Color." *Stanford Law Review* 43, no. 6: 1241–99.

Crenshaw, K., N. Gotanda, G. Peller, and K. Thomas. 1995. *Critical Race Theory: The Key Writings That Formed the Movement*. New York: The New Press.

Cuyjet, Michael J. 2006. *African American Men in College*. San Francisco: Jossey-Bass.

Davenport, Joy Elaine, dir. 2022, February 22. *Fannie Lou Hamer's America: An America Reframed Special*. PBS.

Faulkner, W. 1977. *The Days When the Animals Talked: Black African Folktales and How They Came to Be*. Trenton, NJ: Africa World Press.

Frazier, E. 1939. *The Negro Family in the United States*. Chicago: University of Chicago Press.

Genovese, E. 1972. *Roll Jordan Roll: The World the Slaves Made*. New York: Vintage Books.

Givens, Jarvis. 2021. *Fugitive Pedagogy: Carter G. Woodson and the Art of Black Teaching*. Cambridge: Harvard University Press.

Gomez, M. 1998. *Exchanging Our Country Marks: The Transformation of African Identities in the Colonial and Antebellum South*. Chapel Hill: University of North Carolina Press.

Herskovits, Melville. 1941. *The Myth of the Negro Past*. New York: Harper.

Hill Collins, Patricia. 1991. *Black Feminist Thought*. New York: Routledge.

Leslie, Annie Ruth, Kim Brittingham Barnett, Matasha L. Harris, and Charles Adams. 2021. "Advancing the Demarginalization of African American Students." In *The Black Experience and Navigating Higher Education Through a Virtual World*, edited by Kimetta R. Hairston, Wendy M. Edmonds, and Shanetia P. Clark, 73–96. Hershey, PA: IGI Global.

Love, Bettina. 2019. *We Want to Do More Than Survive: Abolitionist Teaching and the Pursuit of Educational Reform*. Boston, MA: Beacon Press.

Nichols, S., and G. Stahl. 2018. "Intersectionality in Higher Education Research: A Systematic Literature Review." *Higher Education Research and Development* 38, no. 6.

Reddick, Richard J., and Katie Ortego Pritchett. 2016. "'I Don't Want to Work in a World of Whiteness': White Faculty and Their Mentoring Relationships with Black Students." *The Journal of the Professoriate* 8, no. 1: 54–81.

Sealey-Ruiz, Yolanda, and Perry Greene. 2011. "Embracing Urban Youth Culture in the Context of Education." *The Urban Review: Issues and Ideas in Public Education* 43, no. 3: 339–57.

Stuckey, Sterling. 1987. *Slave Culture.* New York: Oxford University Press.

Williams, K., J. Coles, and P. Reynolds. 2020. "(Re)Creating the Script: A Framework of Agency, Accountability, and Resisting Deficit Depictions of Black Students in P–20 Education." *The Journal of Negro Education* 89, no. 3.

CHAPTER 11

Latina Identity and Belonging in Academia
Mariela A. Rodríguez

The chapter is framed within a Latina cultural perspective that includes the use of words and phrases in the author's native language, Spanish. This chapter will be divided into the following sections, which represent different phases of her life journey: (1) *Crecimiento* (Growth); (2) *Entendimiento* (Understanding); (3) *Movimiento* (Movement); (4) *Inspiración* (Inspiration); and (5) *Reflección* (Reflection). In addition to using these headings, she explains how these phases of her life have influenced her actions and how they serve to motivate her toward attaining future goals.

CRECIMIENTO (GROWTH)

Mariela was born and raised in a city that sits along the U.S.-Mexico border in the Rio Grande Valley of Texas. She identifies as Latina, having grown up within a Latino family household and community. Her family spoke both Spanish and English at home; thus the value of both languages was understood.

While she grew up with both a mother and father, she was also blessed by the presence of wonderful matriarchs from both maternal and paternal sides of her family. Having so many aunts to count on really shaped Mariela's formative years in growing as a caring and compassionate individual. Their life lessons and work ethic (Gonzales 2019) inspired her to grow into the strong and independent woman that Mariela is today, with the dedication to be of service to others. She seeks to give *gracias* (thanks) to her mom, dad, and *tías* (aunts) for everything that they've done for her!

ENTENDIMIENTO (UNDERSTANDING)

Mariela can't name the exact moment or event in her early years of schooling that led to her understanding of behaviors that led to success. She understood that doing "well" in school included raising her hand to speak, being polite to teachers, and earning "good" grades (Aragon 2018; Lechuga-Peña and Lechuga 2018). These behaviors were often reinforced by gold stars.

On the familial side, her doing well in school reflected her parents' hard work and dedication to helping Mariela earn a "better" life than they had. The question was not *whether* she would attend college but rather *which* college she would attend. She recalled a conversation with her parents about not attending the local university, which was only a few blocks' walking distance from their home; she wanted to enroll in a school out of town that could enhance her "chances" of earning that better life that they dreamed of for her.

Mariela earned a scholarship to a university about five hours away, and off she went. She still remembers the day that her parents drove to the dormitory. It was a nervous time for all of them since her parents had not attended college and were unsure of what to do. University orientation proved beneficial for all three of them (Harper, Zhu, and Marquez Kiyama 2020) About five years later, Mariela earned a degree as an elementary bilingual teacher and returned to her hometown to begin a public school teaching career. After that, she earned two master's degrees, then was selected through a W. K. Kellogg grant to earn a PhD in full-time research study coupled with a teaching assistantship at an institution out of state. All that stemmed from her early understanding of the benefits that came from getting "good" grades in school.

MOVIMIENTO (MOVEMENT)

In her last year of the doctoral program, Mariela took a position as a non-tenure-track instructor back in her hometown, at the local university that was mentioned previously. She found that position so valuable in her introduction to academia. So many people in the department and college were kind and helpful. Mariela remains friends with some of them, even though almost twenty years have passed since their time as colleagues together. This was a time when she also grew as a "teacher," understanding the importance of being an advisor and mentor to students.

After earning her PhD, Mariela sought a tenure-track position in a different city. While it was difficult to leave the "home" environment, both familial and professional, she embarked on a new journey where she has thrived for the last eighteen years. At this Hispanic-serving institution, Mariela has progressed from assistant professor, to associate professor with tenure, to full professor. She has also served in a variety of leadership roles that have shaped her professional practice, and she has held leadership positions within national organizations.

Life in academia is rife with structural challenges to persons of color (POC), given the longstanding traditions of the "ivory tower," and challenges for Latinas in the academy are evidenced daily (Reyes et al. 2021; Rivera 2021). As a Latina having earned the highest rank in academia, it is a feat that Mariela does not take lightly. The percentages of Latina full professors are small when compared to their White female counterparts (Flores 2020; Gonzales and Saldivar 2020). She understands that she must give back and support others who are also on a similar trajectory. Mariela seeks to do whatever she can to provide opportunities for growth and to lend a listening ear. She knows that she did not reach her professional goals on her own.

INSPIRACIÓN (INSPIRATION)

There is a saying in Spanish: "*Dime con quien andas y te diré quien eres*" ("Tell me with whom you walk, and I'll tell you who you are"). It is reflective of the adage of being judged by the company you keep. This was inculcated into Mariela during her formative years. Her family members continuously emphasized the value of the friends that she made, helping to ensure that the personal and professional relationships that she established were for her *bien* (good), and not to steer her onto a negative path.

It is important to participate in professional and social circles that enhance your energy and help you grow within your best self. Surround yourself with friends and colleagues who help to inspire you. In turn, you will find yourself inspiring others (Camargo Gonzalez 2020).

One most often identifies mentors through professional networks. For Latinas, the importance of such networks is key (López et al. 2021). Mariela considers herself lucky to have been mentored from selfless and giving individuals who inspire her to this day. She had mentors who crossed her path during her academic journey and life-long mentors whom she calls on often; most of them are also Latinas. Mariela has learned valuable lessons from her mentors that help her to be a mentor to others. Mariela considers herself to be sincere, communicative, and caring. These are not only actions that she learned from her mentors but also actions that she cultivated throughout her personal experiences, academic journey, and professional work. By being her true self with those who have invited her to mentor them, Mariela is able to share pieces of herself that yield trust and respect. And she is able to grow from these shared experiences.

REFLECCIÓN (REFLECTION)

So what has Mariela learned so far about mentoring relationships? She's learned that she is truly blessed to have such supportive individuals around her. Each of them helps her to become a better mentor. She hopes that she models valuable behaviors with the mentees that she works with so that they can also grow as mentors to others.

Mariela learned that she must be sincere in her interactions, acknowledging her own fears and vulnerabilities. A mentor is not expected to represent perfection, for that is unattainable to all, and one will be miserable in seeking it. Showing vulnerability is a sign of humanity and resilience of spirit. This honest reflection of self demonstrates to mentees that mentors grow alongside them, and not that mentors are the sages with all of the correct answers. Among Latina scholars, mentoring plays a critical role not only in career advancement but also in providing sustaining support (Acevedo-Gil and Madrigal Garcia 2018).

Mariela would not be where she is professionally without the assistance of various mentors along the way. She will continue to benefit from mentors' advice and actions throughout the rest of her career. She hopes to never believe that she "arrived" on her own. She looks around to those who have assisted her. She looks around to those whom she can assist. Then, together, they will all continue to move forward.

Each of the phases that Mariela has lived, so far, have been filled with experiences that have shaped who she is as a person, how she interacts with others, and the ways that mentors helped set a path for future goals to be realized. While Mariela presented the phases in a linear fashion within this chapter, they should not be interpreted as a step-by-step process that she followed. Mariela continuously engages in moments of growth, inspiration, and reflection throughout her academic and professional journey. Consider the phases as concentric circles that not only influence each other but also are malleable and flexible, expanding and contracting as we proceed along our paths (see figure 11.1).

Mariela placed *reflección* (reflection) outside the concentric circles because one must practice self-reflection throughout each phase of

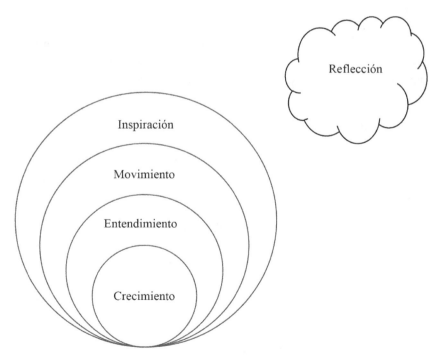

Figure 11.1. Phases of Growth. **Source: *Created by Mariela A. Rodríguez.***

one's life. Engaging in self-reflection offers opportunities to learn from both missteps and successes. Mariela encourages all to seek effective ways to practice self-reflection for that honest look within themselves and at the consequences of their actions.

As Mariela continues in her *crecimiento* (growth) as a Latina scholar in academia, she moves forward filled with hope. This hope is rooted in a need to continue seeking mentors while serving as a mentor for others. Mentorship is truly an act of service. Mariela doesn't just refer to the time that mentoring relationships take, but more to the approach that mentors must have when approaching such relationships.

Being a mentor is not the "green light" to tell others how they should live their lives, or which career path they should follow. Instead, going into a mentoring relationship with a service approach allows the mentor to engage the mentee in what the mentee wants to gain from the relationship. A service approach offers mentees opportunities to explore and reflect on their own growth experiences while the mentor facilitates such exploration and reflection. Mariela strongly believes that the service approach provides meaningful exchanges between mentors and mentees that positively benefit each member of the mentoring relationship. She encourages one to provide the support to others in their mentoring role, but to also learn from each interaction with mentees so that all involved can continue evolving personally and professionally.

REFERENCES

Acevedo-Gil, Nancy, and Yanira Madrigal Garcia. 2018. "Mentoring Among Latina/o Scholars: Enacting Spiritual Activism to Navigate Academia." *American Journal of Education* 124: 313–34.

Aragon, Antonette. 2018. "Achieving Latina Students: Aspirational Counterstories and Critical Reflections on Parental Community Cultural Wealth." *Journal of Latinos and Education* 17, no. 4: 373–85.

Camargo Gonzalez, Lorena. 2020. "'The Weight We Carry in Our Backpack Is Not the Weight of Our Books, It's the Weight of our Community': Latinas Negotiating Identity and Multiple Roles." *InterActions: UCLA Journal of Education and Information Studies* 16, no. 1: 1–29.

Flores, Lisa Y. 2020. "From the Borderland to the Midland: A Latina's Journey into Academia." *Women & Therapy* 43, nos. 1–2: 44–57.

Gonzales, Leslie D., and Guadalupe Saldivar. 2020. "A Systematic Review of Select Social Science and Humanities Literature: The Presence and Positioning of Latina Professors." *Journal of Hispanic Higher Education* 19, no. 2: 118–33.

Gonzales, Sandra M. 2019. "Cultivating *Familismo*: Belonging and Inclusion in One Latina/o Learning Community." *International Journal of Inclusive Education* 23, no. 9: 937–49.

Harper, Casandra Elena, Hao Zhu, and Judy Marquez Kiyama. 2020. "Parents and Families of First-Generation College Students Experience Their Own College Transition." *The Journal of Higher Education* 91, no. 4: 540–64.

Lechuga-Peña, Stephanie, and Chalane E. Lechuga. 2018. "Xicanisma/o and Education: Counter Storytelling and Narratives to Inform Latina/o Student Success." *Journal of Women and Social Work* 33, no. 3: 300–316.

López, Ruth M., Maria L. Honey, Hope S. Pacheco, and Esmeralda C. Valdez. 2021. "*Creando Comunidad*: Experiences of Latina Faculty and Staff Mentors at a Hispanic-Serving Institution." *Journal of Women and Gender in Higher Education* 14, no. 1: 100–120.

Reyes, Ganiva, Veronica R. Barrios, Racheal M. Banda, Brittany Aronson, Esther M. Claros Berlioz, and Martha E. Castañeda. 2021. "We Came Together Out of Necessity: A Latina Diaspora Group Engaging in Plática to Thrive with Dignity in Academia. *Journal of Women and Gender in Higher Education* 14, no. 3: 283–301.

Rivera, Jessica. 2021. "Who Belongs in Academia?" In *Elevating Marginalized Voices in Academe: Lessons for a New Generation of Scholars*, edited by Emerald Templeton, Bridget H. Love, and Onda Johnson. New York: Routledge.

Part IV

THRIVING . . . NOT JUST SURVIVING

I Ain't Sorry
Establishing Boundaries in the Pursuit of Wholeness with JOY
Brandi Hinnant-Crawford

On Beyoncé's infamous visual album *Lemonade*, one of many instantaneous hits was the track titled "Sorry." In the interlude before the song begins, Beyoncé asks, "So what are you going to say at my funeral now that you've killed me?" For many women of color, life in the academy is analogous to being in a toxic relationship where academia is the partner that only takes while the sister-scholar is the one doing all the giving.

As *Lemonade* tells a story, the track "Sorry" shows a shift from being hurt and concerned about the partner's needs and behaviors to centering oneself and one's own needs and desires. As Beyoncé names the things she is going to do for her own good that the partner may not like, the background vocals chant, "I ain't sorry" and "I ain't thinking 'bout you." This chapter is not an analysis of *Lemonade* (though I would suggest you read the *Lemonade* syllabus by sister-scholar Candice Benbow, who has her own tale about toxicity in academia); this chapter is about sister-scholars establishing boundaries so they remain more than scholars—whole women in the midst of a profession that takes more than it gives.

Evangeline Jones Artis Isler (the author's late maternal grandmother) frequently told her daughter and granddaughters, "You got to love self, first." Boundaries are about loving and protecting oneself. Black feminist Brittney Cooper explains that "loving oneself in a world where there is always someone ready to do you harm" (Cooper 2019) is hard, but sister-scholars have provided guidance on how to love oneself without apology. Grounded in Black feminist epistemology (Hill

Collins 2000), which draws meaning from experience, assesses knowledge through dialogue, espouses an ethic of caring, and acknowledges personal responsibility, this chapter describes a three-part framework to guide sister-scholars in setting boundaries within the academy.

Pursuing wholeness is a never-ending journey. Love (2019) explains, "The goal is to be whole." When a sister-scholar is whole and well, her best self emerges. Being her best self allows her to better serve her family, community, institution, and her individual purpose. This chapter presents a framework, titled JOY, to help sister-scholars establish clear boundaries in the pursuit of wholeness. Wholeness comes from self-love and self-care. Wholeness means a life that has purpose, balance, rest, and joy.

Brittney Cooper (2019) explains, "Joy arises from an internal clarity about our purpose" (274). Cooper goes on to reveal the cost of not having joy is "diminished capacity for self-love and self-valuing" (275). Love (2019) describes joy as a necessity, because "joy provides a type of nourishment that is needed to be dark and fully alive in White spaces, such as schools. . . . Black joy is often misunderstood. Black joy is to embrace your full humanity, as the world tells you that you are disposable and that you do not matter" (120). Sister-scholars deserve wholeness and joy.

WHY DO WE NEED A FRAMEWORK FOR ESTABLISHING BOUNDARIES?

While this chapter may speak to all minoritized women, it is grounded in scholarship on Black women. Black women have always had to resist gendered stereotypes within the workplace—historical ones such as the Mammy, Sapphire, and Jezebel, and contemporary ones such as the Crazy Black Bitch and the Superwoman (Reynolds-Dobbs, Thomas, and Harrison 2008). These stereotypes follow Black women into academia. Mammies are loyal, self-sacrificing, and nurturing. "Academic mammying" is defined by Hills (2019) as "a mechanism of mistreatment prompted by the burdensome levying of undue expectation (or under-expectation) on Black women scholars' performance, embodiment, and competence," a phenomenon that is often exacerbated in Predominantly White Institutions (PWIs).

Yet hooks (2001) warns sister-scholars, "We must choose a healthy model of female agency and self-actualization, one rooted in the understanding that when we love ourselves well (not in a selfish or narcissistic way), we are best able to love others. When we have healthy self-love, we know that individuals in our lives who demand of us self-destructive martyrdom do not care for our good" (41). The institution does not love the sister-scholar, so it is critical that the sister-scholar loves herself and sets boundaries for the institution.

The superwoman trope can be just as dangerous for the sister-scholar as the self-sacrificing role of mammy. The superwoman is characterized as highly educated and not possessing the same "fears, weakness, and insecurities" of other women (Reynolds-Dobbs et al. 2008, 138). Reynolds-Dobbs and associates (2008) explain that she is expected to do it all, often with little support. The author views her experience as being in this category, and offers for examination summaries from the three main portions of her dossier submitted for tenure and promotion:

- *On teaching*: When submitting her dossier for tenure and promotion, the author had taught fifty-three courses, an average of 8.8 annually, when her course load was 3/3. She also chaired nine dissertations and served as methodologist on another twenty committees.
- *On scholarship*: For tenure and promotion to associate professor, her department required fifteen scholarship units, nine of which had to be from category A (peer-reviewed journal articles, grants, books). She had accumulated seventy-four scholarship units, twenty-seven from category A, forty-two from category B, and five from category C. This was three times what was required from category A, and nearly five times the overall requirement.
- *On service*: Her department required thirty service units, and that they be spread across internal and external service. The author had accumulated fifty-five service units—nearly twice what was required.

While applauded and unanimously affirmed at the departmental, college, and university collegial review committees, being superwoman led to exhaustion and shortcomings in other areas of the author's life.

While a solo-authored book in the file is heralded as a major contribution to the field, if one reads the acknowledgments, they find apologies: "Elizabeth and Elijah, to whom I feel like I constantly have to apologize for being preoccupied with work . . . I appreciate the grace you give me, as a single career-mom, who cannot be in all places at all times" (Hinnant-Crawford 2020, xiv).

Yet her children are not the only people who deserve an apology. Amid achieving these dossier highlights, during six years of working toward tenure, this single woman went on two dates while partnership was on her vision board each year. Relationships with her girlfriends were strained due to her constant busyness. In being superwoman on the job, sister-scholars shortchange themselves in life. Yet, amid a global pandemic, one realizes the tenure file and curriculum vita cannot come first. Instead of hustling and doing *all the things*, sister-scholars must align—in order to have both balance and joy within the work they are doing.

TASKS, ASSIGNMENTS, AND OPPORTUNITIES

Time, energy, and mental capacity are not just for work. bell hooks (2014) reminds sister-scholars that their foremothers reserved energy for the homeplace—where they created an anti-oppressive enriching space for their families to counter the harsh world outside. Time, energy, and mental capacity are precious resources that must be budgeted like money. Setting boundaries is conscientiously preserving time, energy, and mental capacity—it is not being selfish. Tasks, assignments, and opportunities cost. One must constantly review their internal budget to see if they have enough resources before taking tasks on, considering that their balance should never be zero.

Tasks are short-term responsibilities that may include writing a report or serving as the host for a guest speaker. Tasks in and of themselves are not problematic, until a sister-scholar has accepted too many. While small in nature, they are costly for a short period. Assignments are long-term responsibilities such as membership or leadership of a committee or an administrative position. Assignments are often required but should be curated such that they are not extraneous to a sister-scholar's purpose.

Opportunities are often packaged as shiny and exciting, but that packaging may cause a sister-scholar to miss the cost that is required for the opportunity. Opportunities can be short or long term, such as a grant project, collaborating with stars in the field, or professional development.

PURSUING WHOLENESS WITH JOY

Tasks, assignments, and opportunities will constantly be presented to sister-scholars, and they must be filtered through a barometer of JOY. The following framework uses the mnemonic device *JOY* to help sister-scholars remember four questions to ask themselves before committing to tasks, assignments, and opportunities.

J—Is It Just? Is It Justified?

When presented with a task, opportunity, or assignment, the first thing women of color in the academy should ask is whether or not it is just. While it is unfair that women of color, especially Black women, are expected to be the moral compass of this society, sister-scholars have to begin with the question: Is this *right*? The intersecting oppressions faced by women of color often allow them to see and identify with those who are marginalized and minoritized, and with that degree of visual clarity comes responsibility.

When something is presented to a sister-scholar that may unintentionally hurt students, junior scholars, entry-level student affairs professionals, or anyone else in the academic universe, a sister-scholar should not take on that task, and when necessary, must stand in opposition to it.

Some tasks and assignments require a different question: Is it justified? On occasion, sister-scholars may need to revisit their job descriptions so they are clear what is part of the job and what is beyond it. If a sister-scholar is a tenured or tenure-track faculty member, there are expectations for scholarship, teaching, and service. Office hours are justified because they are a part of teaching. However, if a sister-scholar is an adjunct, service on multiple committees may not be justified. Sister-scholars must also avoid being punished because of their skillsets. Just because she served well in a particular capacity does not mean that task becomes hers in perpetuity.

O—Will This Help Me Meet My Objectives?

As stated earlier, Cooper defines *joy* in part as having clarity of purpose. When presented with tasks, assignments, and opportunities, sister-scholars must ask, "Will this help me meet *my* objectives?" If a sister-scholar is a methodologist, she may be approached to collaborate on a number of different research projects, but her skill does not mean she should accept every invitation. Is the project related to her own research agenda or interest? If not, she should respectfully decline the invitation.

Evaluating your objectives in relation to opportunity also includes opportunities that come with financial incentive. When first being exposed to consulting opportunities, the inclination is to say yes to everything because more money is always needed. There are student loans and mortgages to be paid, childcare, and elder support. Yet when a sister-scholar commits to a paying gig that drains her of energy to do what she is called to do, it robs her of joy and breeds exhaustion. The pay becomes too expensive.

In having clarity of purpose, sister-scholars must determine their long- and short-term objectives. Some assignments may help a sister in the long game. While she may not want to be a program director, she may accept the assignment because she knows eventually she wants to go into administration, and this will give her the necessary experience. If a sister-scholar cannot see how a task, assignment, or opportunity aids her in her immediate or long-term objectives, she should say no.

Y—Is It My Responsibility?

The final question a sister-scholar must ask before adding tasks to her plate is whether or not that task is her responsibility. And for the record, everything related to diversity, equity, and inclusion is not a sister-scholar's responsibility. While sister-scholars, particularly at PWIs, are asked to serve on a variety of committees and taskforces related to DEI, it is not the responsibility of minoritized individuals to dismantle oppressive structures in their academic institutions. In fact, Love (2019) explains, "The fact that dark people are tasked with the work of dismantling these centuries-old oppressions is a continuation of racism" (9).

If there is an all-White taskforce on racism, a sister-scholar may feel compelled to serve to represent minoritized perspectives—the author has done this to her own detriment far too many times. While that perspective may be missing from the taskforce, it is not the sister-scholar's responsibility to correct that problem, especially if the work costs time, energy, and mental capacity. Furthermore, this work comes with an emotional tax; the impact of racial battle fatigue is real (Gorski 2018).

When teaching, sister-scholars must understand the responsibility of the instructor and the responsibility of the student. Being student-centered does not equate to being constantly available. Establishing barriers with students is difficult, especially when sister-scholars are burdened with two minoritized identities that are associated with lower course evaluations (Huston 2005).

Yet, if a sister-scholar is going to succeed at teaching, research, and service, boundaries are necessary, including realistic expectations for grading and feedback, limits on when students can contact the sister-scholar, and a culture of respect in the classroom. Respect looks different to different people; this may mean insisting students use titles (Professor/Dr.) in verbal and written communication.

BOUNDARIES ARE NECESSARY

JOY can help sister-scholars establish boundaries, and boundaries can lead to joy and wholeness. It has become quite popular on social media to quote sister-scholar Audre Lorde (2017) when discussing self-care: "Caring for myself is not self-indulgence, it is self-preservation, and that is an act of political warfare" (130). But prior to this very statement, she identifies the consequences of overextension. Lorde (2017) warns in her own self-reflection—during her battle with cancer: "I had to examine, in my dreams as well as in my immune-function tests, the devastating effects of overextension. Overextending myself is not stretching myself. I had to accept how difficult it is to monitor the difference. Necessary for me as cutting down on sugar. Crucial. Physically. Psychically" (130).

Boundaries are necessities; boundaries are self-care and self-preservation. Boundaries are necessary for joy and wholeness. It is the responsibility of the sister-scholar to develop boundaries. Even if she is superwoman, she does not need to fly all the time. She must ask herself the questions: Is it just? Is it justified? Does it serve my objectives? Is it my responsibility? And when the answer to the questions is no, the sister-scholar must say no—and not be sorry about it.

REFERENCES

Cooper, Brittney C. 2019. *Eloquent Rage: A Black Feminist Discovers Her Superpower*. New York: Picador.

Gorski, Paul C. 2018. "Racial Battle Fatigue and Activist Burnout in Racial Justice Activists of Color at Predominantly White Colleges and Universities." *Race Ethnicity and Education* 22, no. 1: 1–20.

Hill Collins, Patricia. 2000. *Black Feminist Thought: Knowledge, Consciousness, and the Politics of Empowerment*. 2nd ed. London: Routledge.

Hills, Darrius D'wayne. 2019. "'Admirable or Ridiculous?': The Burdens of Black Women Scholars and Dialogue in the Work of Solidarity." *Journal of Feminist Studies in Religion* 35, no. 2: 5–21.

Hinnant-Crawford, B. 2020. *Improvement Science in Education: A Primer*. Gorham, ME: Myers Education Press.

hooks, bell. 2001. *Salvation: Black People and Love*. New York: Harper Perennial.

hooks, bell. 2014. *Yearning: Race, Gender, and Cultural Politics*. New York: Routledge.

Huston, Therese A. 2005. "Race and Gender Bias in Higher Education: Could Faculty Course Evaluations Impede Further Progress toward Parity?" *Seattle J. Soc. Just.* 4, no 2: 591–611.

Lorde, Audre. 2017. *A Burst of Light: And Other Essays*. Mineola, NY: Dover.

Love, Bettina L. 2019. *We Want to Do More Than Survive: Abolitionist Teaching and the Pursuit of Educational Freedom*. Boston, MA: Beacon Press.

Reynolds-Dobbs, Wendy, Kecia M. Thomas, and Matthew S. Harrison. 2008. "From Mammy to Superwoman: Images That Hinder Black Women's Career Development." *Journal of Career Development* 35, no. 2: 129–50.

CHAPTER 13

No Crystal Stair
Black Women Reaching Landings and Turning Corners in Library and Information Science
Shamella Cromartie and Shaundra Walker

Library and information science (LIS) is an overwhelmingly homogenous profession. The experiences of Black women in LIS in academia, particularly how their race and gender intersect within an already feminized profession, are underexplored within the literature. While White women's ascent to leadership positions in academic and research libraries and the receipt of other accolades has been celebrated and documented heavily, Black women have not been as heralded for their strides and innovation in the profession.

Though libraries are often idealized as pillowy work environments and bastions of inclusivity and diversity, the reality is that libraries are still often-overwhelmingly White, and many are still driven by dominant White ideologies and even White supremacy. This makes achieving and leading in academic libraries far more difficult for Black women. This autoethnographic chapter explores the experiences of two Black women in senior leadership positions in academic libraries and likens the experience to the Langston Hughes (1922/1995) poem "Mother to Son." In particular, the authors note that this journey into library leadership roles has been no crystal stair.

Well, son, I'll tell you:
Life for me ain't been no crystal stair.
It's had tacks in it,
And splinters,
And boards torn up,
And places with no carpet on the floor—
Bare.

But all the time
I'se been a-climbin' on,
And reachin' landin's,
And turnin' corners,
And sometimes goin' in the dark
Where there ain't been no light.
So boy, don't you turn back.
Don't you set down on the steps
'Cause you finds it's kinder hard.
Don't you fall now—
For I'se still goin', honey,
I'se still climbin',
And life for me ain't been no crystal stair.

First published in 1922, this poem alludes to the dangers and obstacles faced by Black people that are not faced by White people. Relatable and emotional, the poem is representative to the authors as Black women who have matriculated through the ranks of academic libraries and waded through increased surveillance, tone policing, misogynoir, and epistemic violence in their respective organizations.

Thankfully, there exists a growing body of literature that presents the experiences of LIS professionals of color and is a direct affront to the library's ongoing narrative of professed diversity, equity, and inclusion values. This literature, written in the form of counterstories/ counternarratives, is a direct contradiction to the lofty ideals of diversity, equity, and inclusion the profession espouses but that are not readily shown to colleagues of color. This intercultural dialogue gives voice to our collective understanding of the experiences of Black women and people of color working in LIS.

One of the first of this kind, *Untold Stories: Civil Rights, Libraries, and Black Librarianship* (Tucker 1998) was followed by the counterstories told in *Unfinished Business: Race, Equity, and Diversity in Library and Information Science Education* (Wheeler 2005) and *The 21st-Century Black Librarian in America* (Jackson, Jefferson, and Nosakhere 2012). In the 2018 edited text *Pushing the Margins: Women of Color and Intersectionality in LIS* (Chou and Pho 2018), women of color in LIS tell familiar stories of emotional labor, isolation, tokenism, and various discriminatory experiences in libraries as employees and as LIS students and faculty. As a "safe space" for women of color librarians, the text often feels to the authors like reading their own journals. In another edited text, *Diversity and Inclusion in Libraries: A Call to Action and Strategies for Success* (Jones and Murphy 2019), more librarians of color, in particular Black women, continue to note their successes despite continued attempts at marginalization in library environments.

LIS DEMOGRAPHICS + LIS EDUCATION HISTORY

In considering the experiences of Black women in academic libraries, it is helpful to examine the history of the educational systems that prepare them for this work. Like higher education in general, education and preparation for library work developed separately and unequally. Black women first gained access to training for librarianship through an apprenticeship program offered in Louisville, Kentucky, which operated from 1912 to 1926 out of the Louisville Free Public Library's Negro Branch. Through this program, thirty-seven African American women were trained for work in segregated public libraries (Gunn 1989b). While Edward Christopher Williams would become the first professionally trained African American librarian when he earned a certificate from the New York State Library School in 1900, twenty-three years would pass before the first African American female librarian, Virginia Proctor Powell Florence, would receive a similar honor from the Pittsburgh Carnegie Library School (Gunn 1989a). The Oberlin College graduate possessed an impeccable reputation, and no reason could be found to deny her admission.

Florence's experience was an exception, as African American women would not gain access to library education en masse until the opening of the library school at Hampton Institute in 1926. Open only fourteen years, the school was initially established to provide training for Black women to assume positions in college libraries, but by the time it closed in 1939, it had graduated 183 men and women for work in academic, school, and public libraries (Gunn 1989a).

That same year, when the American Library Association (ALA) surveyed library schools on the performance of African American students in their programs, one school responded this way: "While we have every sympathy for the Negro woman student of course no prejudice, we discourage them for trying to enter the _____ School for Library Science or indeed any department of the University, because there is literally no satisfactory place for them to live in _____. We have had, therefore, no Negro graduates since 1936" (Barker and Parsons Jackson 1939, 41).

Two HBCUs emerged as the primary training grounds for Black librarians. The library education program at Atlanta University (now Clark Atlanta University) was established in 1941; a similar program at North Carolina College for Negroes (now North Carolina Central University) began offering a master of library science in 1950. It is worth noting that both authors are graduates of these programs (North Carolina Central University and Clark Atlanta University, respectively).

Nearly one hundred years after the first Black woman earned a degree in library science, Black women in LIS programs at all levels, from staff members to students to faculty members, continue to report discriminatory treatment. According to the *Emporia Gazette*, Angelica Hale, a Black woman and former employee of the Emporia State University Library School, was awarded $64,303 in back pay in 2019 following her compliant of retaliation when her contract was not renewed after she complained about racial discrimination.

Present-day students of color in LIS programs report similar experiences. For example, one student describes their experience this way: "Like this master's program is good at like a lot of things and it's like rewarding, but like that does come to a very personal cost if you are a minority. Like that is straight up what it is. You have to be able to look past and give up, and be quiet" (Soni 2020). It is safe to say that the experiences of Black women within library science education, the academy, and the library profession at large have been and continue to be perilous, uneven, and segregated.

TACKS, SPLINTERS, AND BOARDS TORN UP

Though a proliferation of diversity-related initiatives exists and has sought to increase the number of librarians of color, the authors are unaware of any widespread initiative that addresses retention and promotion, and certainly there are no widespread programming initiatives that address the dangers of library culture for people of color. Advancement through the ranks of LIS mirrors that of the aforementioned descriptors of library education for Black women: perilous, uneven, and separated. The path from library school to library leadership can be accurately described as full of "tacks, splinters and boards torn up," and there is often no blueprint for Black women in library leadership. Further, "the constant messaging Black people in LIS receive is that we need to conform to whiteness and white culture in these spaces" (Jackson and Flash 2021). This makes for a harried ascent into leadership marked by perceived incompetence.

For years, librarians have lamented the lack of diversity in the profession, and a growing number have further lamented the "whiteness" of the profession. Diversity initiatives in libraries continue to receive praise, though seemingly, the needle has not moved in terms of diversity of the profession or the whiteness it protects. Dr. Maurice Wheeler notes that though the profession seems "receptive" to diversity, it has been the "tremendous bravery and foresight" of a few library leaders that has sought the inclusion of Black people as library educators, professionals, and leaders (Wheeler and Smith 2018).

As the authors reflect on similar circumstances in their respective libraries, specifically related to the duality of their identities as Black women in leadership, it is not lost on them that Black women across all industries and professions face similar circumstances. Black women face more microaggressions statistically than any other group. A 2020 survey from the Gallup Center on Black Voices found that Black women are less likely to feel respected or valued in their workplaces. They are also less likely to feel like a valued member of their team and that their coworkers treat everyone fairly (Lloyd 2021). Not only are there consistent "interpersonal expressions of power" from direct reports to contend with, but also there are often attempts to undermine and discord. Relatively, during the COVID-19 pandemic, reports have surfaced that many Black women were "relieved" to work from home as it freed them from the burden of workplace incivility and microaggressions (Lloyd 2021).

REACHIN' LANDINS' AND TURNIN' CORNERS

In the spirit of earlier counternarratives from Black women in LIS, one author shares her experiences in libraries, mostly academic libraries. As a graduate of the last remaining Historically Black College/University (HBCU) with a library science program, the author had high hopes for the profession because of the diversity of her cohort. Though this was not intentionally misleading, it did cause her to mischaracterize the expected diversity of the organizations in which she would be employed after graduation. Though the author would be the "first" Black person in the role in the position in several organizations, it was the leadership role at a predominately White institution that proved most challenging and eye opening regarding the realities of the profession as professed by many before her.

In this particular library, the author was the sole Black employee in the unit and did not have the luxury of a blueprint to follow. True to form, the previous person in the role was a White woman, with whom others in library leadership, except the dean, enjoyed a very close and communicative relationship. The author reflects on her interview process, in which she was asked about "fitting in" at the library and where library employees inappropriately commented that they did not think she would "like living around here." Further, chosen as second in command to another woman of color (the dean), the experience was fraught from the first day with microaggressions and immediate challenges to her competence, and continued challenges to her leadership. Though the dean was not a Black woman, it certainly seemed that she was being punished for choosing a Black woman for this leadership role.

The Center for Community Organizations' (2019) adapted and revised guide on "White Supremacy Culture in Organizations" notes perfectionist culture, individualism, and either/or thinking as some of the tools of White supremacy. The two women of color faced consistent, vague, and manufactured complaints of "transparency," accusations of "secrecy" and "communications concerns," and alleged "skill gaps," in addition to attempts to ostracize, undermine, and antagonize them publicly and privately. These tools, along with others, would prove effective in leading to a change of leadership in the dean's role.

Then, the lone woman of color in the library and in the library's leadership ranks, the author continued to be met with disdain while amplifying the library's visibility on campus, revitalizing library programming, and taking action on the espoused diversity values. In transitioning to an additional supervisory role in the same library, the author faced a peculiar type of misogyny: the more specifically anti-Black-woman type called misogynoir. *Misogynoir* is a term coined by Moya Bailey to articulate "the specific hatred, dislike, distrust, and prejudice directed toward Black women" (quoted in Asare 2020). The author recalls a White man attempting to scold her without cause or provocation immediately upon the date her supervision of him became active. Shortly thereafter, he began a program of change resistance, gossiping, and recruitment to affect her leadership in the department. Though these attempts proved futile, the individual remained passive-aggressive and attempted to use the tools of White supremacy to rattle the author, including gaslighting, tone policing, and defensiveness when called out on this behavior.

PATH TO LEADERSHIP

This coauthor was drawn to the profession at a time when there was an increased focus on diversity. As a graduate of an HBCU, she was drawn to the library education program at Clark Atlanta University (CAU) because it was in the same university system as her undergraduate alma mater. It was also the alma mater of many of the Black women librarians she had encountered in her childhood, particularly her media specialists in K–12 schools and the academic librarians who served her undergraduate library. For her, librarianship was a career in which she could see herself working and leading because she had seen other Black women do the same.

Although her experience in the library education program at Clark Atlanta was overwhelmingly positive, she was introduced to the racial dynamics within the library profession and higher education writ large as she attempted to make the transition from graduate student to professional. For example, when she was nearing the completion of her program and found herself seeking an internship in her hometown, her internship-placement coordinator struggled to find a site for her. This dilemma spoke to the dual system of graduate library education that had existed in the state; the library school at Clark Atlanta was established in 1941 as a school for future African American librarians, while a library school opened at Emory University, also in Atlanta in 1928. Even after the library school at Emory closed in 1990, many White students preferred to attend library school in neighboring states rather than attend Clark Atlanta. As a matter of fact, the state of Georgia offered tuition assistance to these students to attend school out of state.

The coauthor's experience gaining her first professional experience was equally challenging. After one interview at a regional public university in the state, she never received any information about the status of the search, only learning that the position had been given to someone else through a colleague. When she finally secured her first professional position at an academic library, she was extended a "visiting" appointment, a status that she later discovered was unique to her. The visiting appointment was particularly interesting given that librarians at the institution did not hold tenure and only received renewing appointments.

At every institution where she has been employed as a librarian, with the exception of four years spent working at an HBCU library, the coauthor has literally made Black history, as she was the first Black librarian in each school's history. To contextualize this fact, readers should be reminded that the coauthor has worked exclusively in Georgia, home of a library education program that graduated more Black librarians than any other ALA-accredited program in the nation. In addition to serving as the first Black librarian at two institutions of higher education, the coauthor holds the distinction of being the first Black librarian to earn tenure in the history of her current institution. Although this achievement serves as a point of pride, it has not come without challenges and obstacles. These experiences beg the question: How is it that in a state with a school that has produced more Black librarians than any other, a school could employ its first Black librarian in the year 2002? Why did it take over one hundred years for an institution to tenure its first Black librarian?

Presently, the coauthor is the most highly credentialed and most experienced librarian at her current institution, yet she is often met with surprise when introduced as the library director. As she progressed toward tenure and promotion to associate professor, the coauthor was intentional about going above and beyond the tenure and promotion requirements, listening to the mantra that is instilled into many a Black child, that they must work extra hard and go above and beyond what is expected. This resulted in a publication and national presentation every year prior to applying for promotion and tenure.

This coauthor has also found that her praxis, which can be described as critical librarianship, has not come without challenge. Critical librarianship interrogates the library and information science as social and political institutions. With that in mind, her scholarship and service have focused on race within library and information science, with particular emphasis on the recruitment, retention, and promotion of librarians of color. Her tenure and promotion portfolios were described as "interesting," but most importantly and significantly, in the tradition of Black women librarians like Virginia Proctor Powell Florence, they were undeniable.

I'SE STILL CLIMBIN'

Whereas resilience narratives are popular, the authors seek to contribute to the tradition of "calling out transgressions" in LIS. For certain, the authors have suffered through unfortunate discriminatory experiences in their rise to library leadership but have emerged as influential library leaders and innovators despite the "culture of academia." More of the master's tools—including weaponized collegiality, bureaucracy, and inequitable and unequal tenure and promotion processes—have been no match for tenacity, skill, and competence.

Both librarians represented are award-winning librarians with both regional and national accolades under their belts and expect to continue to thrive in the profession. To borrow from Anna Julia Cooper, the coauthors have rejected the resilience narrative that permeates the LIS profession, preferring instead to decide when and where they enter.

REFERENCES

Asare, Janice Gassam. 2020, September 22. "Misogynoir: The Unique Discrimination That Black Women Face." *Forbes*. www.forbes.com/sites/janicegassam/2020/09/22/misogynoir-the-unique-discrimination-that-black-women-face/?sh=4376752456ef.

Barker, Tommi Dora, Evalene Parsons Jackson, and the American Library Association. 1939. *Memorandum on the Need in the South for a Library School or Schools for Negroes*. Chicago, IL: American Library Association, Board of Education for Librarianship.

Center for Community Organizations. 2019. *White Supremacy Culture in Organizations*. https://coco-net.org/wp-content/uploads/2019/11/Coco-WhiteSupCulture-ENG4.pdf.

Chou, Rose L., and Annie Pho. 2018. *Pushing the Margins: Women of Color and Intersectionality in LIS*. Sacramento, CA: Library Juice Press.

Gunn, Arthur C. 1989a. "Early Training for Black Librarians in the US: A History of the Hampton Institute Library School and the Establishment of the Atlanta University School of Library Service." Doctoral dissertation, University of Pittsburgh.

Gunn, Arthur C. 1989b, February 1. "The Struggle of Virginia Proctor Powell Florence: A Black Woman Wants to Be a Professional," *American Libraries* 20, no. 2: 154–57.

Hughes, Langston. 1922/1995. "Mother to Son." In *The Collected Poems of Langston Hughes*, edited by Arnold Rampersad and David Roessel, 621. New York: Alfred A. Knopf.

Jackson, Andrew P., Julius Jefferson Jr., and Akilah Nosakhere. 2012. *The 21st-Century Black Librarian in America: Issues and Challenges*. Lanham, MD: Scarecrow Press.

Jackson, Lorin, and Kenya Flash. 2021, October 26. "Surveillance and Captivity of Black Excellence under the White Gaze: What the Treatment of Black Celebrities Can Tell Us about Black Librarianship." WOC+lib. www.wocandlib.org/features/2021/10/26/surveillance-and-captivity-of-black-excellence.

Jones, Shannon D., and Beverly Murphy. 2019. *Diversity and Inclusion in Libraries: A Call to Action and Strategies for Success*. Lanham, MD: Rowman & Littlefield.

Lloyd, Camille. 2021, March 5. "Black Women in the Workplace." Gallup. www.gallup.com/workplace/333194/black-women-workplace.aspx.

Soni, Karina. 2020. "Walking on Eggshells: Experiences of Students of Color within Library and Information Science Master's Programs." Master's thesis, University of North Carolina–Chapel Hill.

Tucker, John Mark. 1998. *Untold Stories: Civil Rights, Libraries, and Black Librarianship*. Urbana-Champaign: Graduate School of Library and Information Science, University of Illinois.

Wheeler, Maurice B. 2005. *Unfinished Business: Race, Equity, and Diversity in Library and Information Science Education*. Lanham, MD: Scarecrow Press.

Wheeler, Maurice B., and Daniella Smith. 2018. "Race and Leadership in Library and Information Science Education: A Study of African American Administrators." *Library Trends* 67, no. 1: 23–38.

CHAPTER 14

Triple Threat
Thriving as a Black Woman Mathematician
Dandrielle Lewis

Thriving. This author's course as a Black female mathematician began while teaching and doing research with undergraduates, resulting in the purpose of her work being set: to create opportunities and access for people. The author did not know her journey would lead her to this rare opportunity to reflect and share a portion of her story on how she is advancing in higher education. She is still aspiring for greater advancement and leadership roles. When asked to write a contributing chapter, she wondered what she could possibly add to the advice and strategies presented in this amazing work by phenomenal authors and leaders in higher education. She decided that a presentation of her experiences, her story, and strategies she is learning along the way will represent advancement and thriving through her life's lens.

The voice reflected in this manuscript solely reflects the author's experiences and is not meant to represent all Black female mathematicians who have experienced traumas and successes in higher education. Their stories are their own, and they deserve to be heard as well. When asked, "Once success is achieved, how do I reach back and make sure I guide aspiring novice educators through the process?" this author's response is with this contribution, with mentoring, with continuing to enter spaces where diverse perspectives need to be heard, and with providing guidance along the way, not just when success is achieved.

The phrase *three strikes* is used in baseball to indicate being out, with no more attempts. For some it means three transgressions, infractions, or mistakes. In this context, the term *strike* will be used as it is in baseball. A triple threat is a person who is proficient in three important skills within their field. Instead of using the word *threat*, *talent* (a special ability that allows a person to do something well) will be used.

This narrative is presented in three parts: "The Perfectionist," "Impostor Syndrome," and "The Only One." In each part, the author discusses a strike and a talent that led to lessons learned and strategies on how to navigate higher education through her lens as a Black woman mathematician.

STRATEGIES FOR NAVIGATING ACADEMIA

At each stage of her career, from high school to her current position as a department chair, the author has remained authentic through preparation, passion, embracing all her imperfections, remaining humble, and being committed to learning and staying relevant. Great mentoring helps her turn fear of failure into opportunities to grow and take risks. Reflection helps her see that the strikes also work in her favor. Here are some recommended strategies to use in navigating higher education and pursuing advancement:

- Plan by creating short-term and long-term goals.
- Plan for the unexpected, and be able to adjust to the detours of life. Networking, making connections, and building relationships with people in and out of your discipline are valuable.
- Remain true to who you are, and pursue your passions.
- *Dream.* If you want it, do the work, and go get it! Don't let anyone stop you.
- Find your people, and create and nurture your support system. Look for those who support you. For example, if you are the best in your circle, you need to expand your circle because you need to be around people who are going to push you and inspire you to greater levels.
- Good mentors are important. The author works in a male-dominated discipline, and she had male mentors. Your mentors may not be of the same gender or race, and they may even be in a different field. Mentors outside of the author's field have been essential to her pursuit of advancing to higher administrative positions.

- Know the rules and the guidelines for every endeavor. Then push the boundaries. The "Impostor Syndrome" section provides guidance on learning the rules.
- Be disciplined. Be strategic. Be focused.
- Cultivate your gift. Engage and participate in experiences that stretch you and help you grow.
- Do the things that make you feel good!
- Use your voice. Even if it is shaky, it matters!
- Balance life and work, and enjoy the journey.
- Life is more than surviving; it's about thriving.

Thriving means bringing your full self to the spaces you occupy and making forward progress, to positively impact those around you, your academic community, and the world.

Throughout this narrative, thriving is connected to locations, learning, growth, access, achievement, advancement, and administration. Now come on this journey as the author shares how she learned the strategies that have helped her thrive.

For the author, math has always been an outlet—the one thing that would work outright if she figured out how to solve the problem or manipulate the equation. Using more than one approach to get a desired result was beautiful and captivating, and it still is! But why did she need an outlet?

PART I: THE PERFECTIONIST

The right mentor, will give you a level of audacity that you better be prepared to do something with. —Felecia Hatcher

The author grew up in a home as the baby girl in a family where her mama was a seamstress and her daddy was a machinist. She had two older sisters and a younger brother. Her father used fear to control her. Her mother used love, hope, education, work ethic, and religion to inspire her, to encourage her to dream, and to show her how to be a good person. As a teenager, failing meant she would be stuck in a small town where the biggest opportunity was working at a hog plant. It also meant being stuck in a place where her daddy would control her.

So fear of failure was motivation. She was determined not to fail. Mama always told her to "get your education and be you no matter where you are and where you go." To this day, her mother still tells her to "be you because it's gotten you this far." The author's mother encouraged her to be authentic. *Fear of failure (Strike 1)* and *authenticity (Talent 1)* helped her become the straight-A student in high school who was well rounded and outgoing—the perfectionist.

The decision to pursue math at Winston Salem State University, a Historically Black College/University (HBCU), was a no-brainer because her older sisters went to school there, and the school was located about three hours from her home, so there would be freedom—freedom to explore the math that she loved and freedom to get involved with new experiences, while meeting new people. This was one of the best and most exciting decisions of her life. After completing her junior year, in summer 2000 she interned with the Quality Education for Minorities (QEM) Network and the National Science Foundation (NSF).

She began this experience knowing she wanted to work in industry when she completed her undergraduate degree because teachers didn't make enough money. This life-changing internship experience shifted the trajectory of her career in mathematics. She was exposed to people with doctorates in STEM who looked like her, and she had the entire summer to network with them and engage in research and professional development opportunities, while also having a lot of fun in Washington, DC.

She learned early on that life-work balance is extremely important. She worked 8 a.m. to 5 p.m. After 5 p.m., she decompressed with friends, went on adventures in the city, and planned fun activities on the weekend. Living her life and being happy is a priority. As she advances, she finds it more challenging to balance life and work, but incorporating self-care is important and necessary.

Dr. Shirley McBay, a pioneering mathematician and founder and president of QEM, was the first Black person to receive a doctorate from the University of Georgia, and she was a leading voice for diversity in science and math education (Risen, 2021). On the first day of the author's internship, the cohort of interns met with Dr. McBay and board members in a boardroom at QEM. The author vividly remembers

Dr. McBay entering the room wearing her suit, smiling, welcoming the interns, and commanding their attention solely with her presence and demeanor. The author's first thought was "Wow!! She's in charge here, and she looks like me!" That day she told the interns they would keep a portfolio of their experience; she communicated her expectations of them, and she gave them their mentor pairings and assignments with deadlines.

In the author's portfolio, she had to include a short-term and long-term career plan, three- and five-year plans, respectively. In her long-term plan, she included becoming successful and having fun doing it, and she included starting a program for minorities in math to give back to her community and to show young Black folks that you can have fun doing math.

Dr. McBay and a host of other lifelong mentors the author gained from NSF during the summer 2000 internship modeled leadership, knowledge, wisdom, representation, and voice in decision-making spaces that she had never entered or dreamed of before that experience. They also modeled successful navigation of being Black with a PhD in higher education. That summer, they showed this author that she could achieve all of this! To advance, however, getting her PhD had to be the next step.

Strike 1: Fear of Failure

Although the author had fears of failure, she never experienced major failure until she was in graduate school at the University of Iowa (UI), a Predominately White Institution. During her first year, she learned math was more than computation. In fact, there was theoretical and abstract math, which was not natural to her, but she was always up for a challenge to enhance her skills and to learn. Effective study habits from undergrad were not as effective in grad school, so she had to learn how to learn higher-level math.

She owes the math skills she gained to Dr. Phil Kutzko and Sharon Lima, a friend and fellow graduate student, who taught her how to learn math. A study session with Sharon lasted a few hours, and it consisted of dissecting the statement of a major theorem, understanding each term introduced, proving the theorem, and working through many examples, followed by presentations to illustrate understanding. These sessions—coupled with the author's work ethic—worked so well for her with abstract algebra that she went on to pass the abstract algebra qualifying exam, one of three exams she needed to pass to begin dissertation research.

After passing the first exam, she started giving back by helping a couple of other graduate students from HBCUs transition to the math program at UI. This experience helped her realize that teaching in college would be the way she could give back and inspire others to pursue math.

Then she took the topology qualifying exam, and she failed it. She came close to passing, but close is not good enough. This was devastating. Perfectionism comes with a lot of self-induced pressure to be flawless and pressure to be the best. Early on, this motivated her to pursue paths that would make her successful, whatever that meant. In that moment, she was not motivated. She ran into a brick wall, and she only had one more attempt to pass the topology qualifying exam.

She failed her second attempt.

This failure meant she would have to leave the PhD program at UI. Some professors told her that she should work at a community college. Other professors told her that she knew more math than required for a PhD. She earned her master's degree from UI, and she had two choices: find a place to work, or find another program to get her PhD. Her lifelong mentors from NSF taught her that a PhD was the ticket to sit at the table and to make decisions that can positively impact the lives of many others to follow. She had to get that ticket, so she chose to find another program. Dr. David Manderscheid, the department chair of math at UI, referred her to Dr. Luise Kappe at Binghamton University, State University of New York (SUNY). Ultimately, that is where the author received her PhD, with Dr. Ben Brewster as her advisor, and she was the first Black person to receive a PhD in the math program at Binghamton University, SUNY.

Her fear of failure became a harsh reality at UI, and she was riddled with self-doubt. Great mentoring and support from her family and lifelong mentors inspired her to continue pursuing her PhD by reminding her of who she was, and that the world needed her and her perspective. At this point in her journey, she learned how to turn her failures into lessons learned and how to make them work to her advantage.

Talent 1: Authenticity

The ability to turn failure into an opportunity takes creativity, intentionality, and focus.

Throughout her journey, the author has learned how to effectively apply her experiences to other challenges in her life, improving herself at each level of advancement. She has a strong work ethic. She loves problem-solving, creating opportunities, and strategic planning. She likes engaging in and creating experiences that are multi-purposed and cross disciplines. What makes this authentic is she learned how to simultaneously do this for both students and faculty, serving the latter with inspiration, motivation, and enriching research and professional development opportunities.

Twelve years after the summer 2000 internship, as a budding mathematician and in her second year post-PhD, at the University of Wisconsin–Eau Claire (UWEC), the author and Dr. Carolyn Otto created a Sonia Kovalevsky high school and middle school math day for girls. The author's dream program happened collaboratively and in a different community, but it happened! The main goal of this program is to increase the representation of women and women from historically underrepresented groups in math. The creation of this sustained program helps progress diversity in STEM. Including a research component for this program with publishable results counted toward tenure, so it served others, and it also served the author.

Striving for perfection, an unrealistic state that leaves no room for error, motivated her, and as she advances, striving for perfection adds stress. She is not perfect. She is effective, and she is good at doing the things that feel good to her, that she is passionate about, and that serve others. When she began to focus on those things, she began to thrive.

PART II: IMPOSTOR SYNDROME

> For there is always light / If only we're brave enough to see it / If only we're brave enough to be it. —Amanda Gorman

When serving others, it is very easy to lose yourself. The *noise* from others can often deter you from your biggest dreams and desires, causing self-doubt and a sense of not belonging in a space that you have earned a right to occupy. This is impostor syndrome. Personal experience has taught this author that administrative roles come with *noise*, and, at times, this *noise* is loud, powerful, sometimes negative, and distracting. Limiting yourself to empower others is focusing on the *noise* (*Strike 2*). To advance, you must *focus on your own success first*, before you can help others (*Talent 2*).

Talent 2: Focus on Your Success First

Every time you fly, flight attendants tell you to "Please place the mask over your own mouth and nose before assisting others." Advancement in higher education requires you to *put your mask on first* before assisting others (*Talent 2*). To be successful, you have to grind, and do not let the *noise* distract you from your goal. Advance, learn, grow, and repeat. Advance, learn, grow, and repeat.

The author's goal is to leave the world better than she found it. So when she advances and takes on new leadership roles, her goal is to leave the places and people better than she found them. Throughout her career, successful advancement has included achievements and access.

The University of Wisconsin–Eau Claire (UWEC)

UWEC and the leadership there nurtured the author's drive and professionalism. She was given the space, opportunity, and support to learn, grow, and advance. Collaborating with colleagues resulted in developing and leading a sustainable high school and middle school math day for girls, a Somali immersion program in Midwestern public schools, and a Senegal international immersion program for undergraduates. Leading those programs required taking risks in unfamiliar settings, writing successful grant proposals, securing funding, strategic planning, partnership development, vision, execution, and implementation. She was thriving by exploring her passion for developing programs for historically underrepresented groups to create access in mathematical and interdisciplinary research.

Her colleagues nominated her for awards, and she won the UW System Outstanding Woman of Color in Education Award and the

Mathematical Association of America Henry L. Alder Teaching Award. She also won the Winston Salem State University Alumni Achiever Award. These *achievements* were received before tenure. To the author, this is favor beyond measure.

Unknown to her, UWEC leadership was paying close attention. She was invited to speak about her programs in leadership and executive committee meetings, and she began to take on leadership roles at the university. Leadership told her, "We need you and your voice in these rooms." She earned *access* by doing what she loves. Her UWEC experiences taught her to put her mask on first. Her preparation focuses on the details because the details of what you do make you better than everybody else. As a Black woman mathematician, there is no room for error because some consider her very presence to be *noise*.

Leadership training, mentoring, and experience help her learn the rules and the guidelines in advancement—because the learning never stops, even after the advancement. To learn the rules, seek guidance and advice. Find a mentor who knows how to navigate the spaces you desire to occupy. Ask that mentor questions. Apply what you learn to your journey. Make your own informed decisions. Enhance your skillset. Explore and take calculated risks. Do your research. The following books can be helpful:

- Gutiérrez y Muhs et al.'s (2012) *Presumed Incompetent: The Intersections of Race and Class for Women in Academia*;
- Kotter and Rathgeber's (2006) *Our Iceberg Is Melting: Changing and Succeeding under Any Conditions*;
- Covey's (1989) *The Seven Habits of Highly Effective People: Restoring the Character Ethic*;
- Covey and Merrill's (2006) *The Speed of Trust: The One Thing That Changes Everything*;
- McChesney et al.'s (2012) *The 4 Disciplines of Execution: Achieving Your Wildly Important Goals*; and
- Collins's (2001) *Good to Great: Why Some Companies Make the Leap . . . and Others Don't.*

The author has also benefited from conferences for department chairs—to discuss the challenges faced in that position and strategies on navigating the position successfully—and leadership institutes—to learn new leadership skills and grow professionally.

Your journey will not be the same as the author's, so be flexible. Always stay true to who you are and believe in yourself. Her programs always involve exposing all students to renowned mathematicians and leaders from historically underrepresented groups because creating access is a part of her personal mission. Her intentionality for this component provides exposure for budding mathematicians and leaders and creates mentoring opportunities for future educators.

Administration

Two years post-tenure, the author became director of the Liberal Studies program at UWEC, where she learned how to navigate the responsibilities of an administrative role. Her circle expanded, and she received mentoring on how to manage, delegate, create policies, and respond effectively to situations, concerns, and people. One year later, she became the first Black woman department chair of mathematical sciences at a Predominantly White Institution located in the southeastern region of the United States.

Strike 2: The Noise

Her first year as a department chair was filled with excitement, *noise*, exhaustion, stress, and a pandemic. A global pandemic.

In addition to the chair responsibilities, she carried the responsibilities of being the first Black chair and member of the department, which was exhausting. Her personal goal, to empower others and create an environment that allows people to thrive more, was ambitious for an outsider, and in her second semester, she experienced a global pandemic. Mid-semester, faculty and students had to transition to remote learning, and some faculty had to learn how to deliver remote instruction. It took a group effort to survive that moment, and honestly, in higher education, programs and universities are still recovering. Thriving turned into surviving. She became so focused on empowering and encouraging others that she limited herself, which is Strike 2. The *noise* also made her question her decision to become department chair. Pause. Breathe.

Learned lessons: Empowering others should not come at the expense of neglecting your own needs, desires, and wellness. Balance is important. Hearing *noise* should not make you question yourself and your capabilities.

Learning how to effectively navigate programs, supervise, advise students, and provide student opportunities through a pandemic, and remotely, was not just surviving. She was thriving. Departmentally, they were thriving. Perspective is everything. Reflection has helped her see that everyone learning how to deliver remote instruction is a helpful skillset. The needs of faculty and students were seen through a new lens of regular check-ins, the need for community engagement, and space and time for mental wellness. Through this lens, the author realized she was exhausted, and she needed to extend the same grace and self-care to herself.

On the other side of exhaustion, there are many good things. Keep going. There will always be challenges, so be a good problem-solver and learn how to navigate through the challenges.

Almost two years into this pandemic, the department, faculty, faculty research programs, and students are thriving. The author is thriving too as a fellow of a math leadership institute and associate editor of a national math magazine because she made the choice to put her mask on first.

If you are navigating impostor syndrome, build your muscle to carry the things and people that are important to you, endure the difficult days, and enjoy the good days.

Lesson Learned: You can always do more than you think you can.

PART III: THE ONLY ONE

Because you deserve! You deserve to be served well. —Dr. Candice R. Price

The author experienced setbacks and hurdles as she journeyed from being the only one in spaces where she learned, to becoming the only one in spaces where she leads. *Being the only one* in a White-male-dominated discipline is unfamiliar territory (*Strike 3*). Despite the temporary setbacks and hurdles, *choose to add value* (*Talent 3*).

Strike 3: Being the Only One

As the only one in unfamiliar territory, the author has been isolated, disrespected, challenged about her decisions, and unwelcomed to environments. For example, she was told, "We were one big happy family, and then you came." Hearing that comment hurt, and it felt like a dagger being driven into her soul. People tried to break her and her spirit. She learned she cannot control what people think of her, but she can control her reaction and her feelings. Unfortunately, her experience is not unique as a Black woman mathematician (see Gutiérrez y Muhs et al., 2012). She represents change, and that change makes people uncomfortable and afraid. But her diverse perspectives are needed in administrative and STEM spaces, and her support extends beyond these spaces.

For navigating and advancing while being the only one in a space in higher education, these pearls of wisdom are offered:

- Set healthy boundaries. For example, learn how to say no confidently to the things and people that are not aligned with your goals and that are not in the best interest of the mission and vision you made a commitment to uphold.
- Keep your values, and trust your instincts. If something does not feel right, trust that feeling. Do everything within your power to develop fair and just policies that will move the needle forward with progress.
- Find or build a community. People need people. As you advance, the available people may be few and far between, but finding people who you can trust and with whom you can discuss the day-to-day challenges and successes is key to thriving and maintaining balance.
- Document everything. Keep track of meeting dates, times, and content; deadlines; and proof of submissions. Be able to provide insight, evidence, and justification whenever necessary. You must be your best advocate. As a BIPOC woman, you must work twice as hard and be intentional about practicing self-care. It is this author's hope that working twice as hard changes for you, and that her efforts make it easier for those who follow.

- Find advocates. Advocates may be a different gender or ethnicity. Nurture this support system.
- Strategize and plan. Learn the nuances for your position, and plan so that it will help you as you advance and make it easier for the next person to follow.

Talent 3: Choose to Add Value

As First Lady Michelle Obama stated, "When they go low, we go high." Choosing to add value sets you apart from the rest. The author chooses to show up every day as her best self, implementing her best and unique skills for the betterment of her department and university. Years ago, she desired to be where she is today, and she owes it to herself to continue to thrive and strive for excellence. She continues to seek opportunities to improve her leadership skills and enhance her professional development. Improving herself benefits her and those around her with enhanced programs, activities, and strategic approaches.

Lesson Learned: It is not selfish to keep your personal goals while helping and empowering others. Advance, learn, grow, and repeat.

There are many paths to advancement and in this journey called life. It is the author's hope that her story and the shared strategies and lessons learned helps you navigate higher education and beyond. Rooms and spaces are elevated when women of color are in them. Take stands, and do not let anyone make you afraid of your own voice. Be courageous. As you advance, you may experience growing pains, but press through them because they are temporary. Level up by embracing new routines, and define *success* on your own terms. Advance, learn, grow, and repeat.

The author thanks the editors of this book for giving her the opportunity to make this contribution. She also thanks her village—family, mentors, and friends—who read this and provided advice and guidance. She appreciates you rocking and riding with her on her life's journey.

REFERENCES

Collins, James C. 2001. *Good to Great: Why Some Companies Make the Leap . . . and Others Don't*. New York: Harper Business.

Covey, Stephen M. R., and Rebecca R. Merrill. 2006. *The Speed of Trust: The One Thing That Changes Everything*. New York: Free Press.

Covey, Stephen R. 1989. *The Seven Habits of Highly Effective People: Restoring the Character Ethic*. New York: Simon and Schuster.

Gutiérrez y Muhs, Gabriella, Yolanda Flores Niemann, Carmen G. Gonzalez, and Angela P. Harris. 2012. *Presumed Incompetent: The Intersections of Race and Class for Women in Academia*. Logan: Utah State University Press.

Kotter, John P., and Holger Rathgeber. 2006. *Our Iceberg Is Melting: Changing and Succeeding under Any Conditions*. New York: St. Martin's Press.

McChesney, Chris, Sean Covey, and Jim Huling. 2012. *The 4 Disciplines of Execution: Achieving Your Wildly Important Goals*. London: Simon & Schuster.

Risen, Clay. 2021. "Shirley McBay, Pioneering Mathematician, Is Dead at 86." *New York Times*, December 14. www.nytimes.com/2021/12/14/science/shirley-mcbay-dead.html.

CHAPTER 15

Getting Published
A Black Woman's Journey to Tenure and Promotion
Dionne V. McLaughlin

A dearth of literature exists that addresses the experiences of tenured or tenure-track Black women professors. Black women professors are woefully underrepresented in academia. Given that only 2 percent of full professors are Black females, 3 percent are associate professors, and 5 percent are assistant professors nationally at postsecondary institutions, these data support the assertion that the presence of a Black female full, associate, or assistant tenured or tenure-track professor is a rarity. Although an anomaly—Dr. Denise Badger (a pseudonym), a recently tenured associate professor—overcame the odds.

The story of her publishing journey is documented here in hopes of sharing how junior faculty can prioritize publishing, overcome obstacles, and join the ranks of other tenured Black faculty in the academy. Dr. Badger shares tips for publishing her first two books and other publication projects. Dr. Badger is fortunate to have made the acquaintance of several full professors who have been instrumental in her success. The importance of timing and collegial relationships cannot be overstated.

Seven years ago, Dr. Denise Badger, a Black educator, began her second post in higher education as an assistant professor at North Carolina Central University. Her experiences as a former high school and elementary school principal prepared her for work with aspiring school leaders. She realized the importance of scholarship, so she prioritized writing to ensure adequate annual progress toward reappointment, promotion, and tenure.

Tenure at the university level is typically conferred upon successful completion of agreed-on department, school, and university tenure and promotion standards of teaching, scholarship, and service. Junior faculty most often begin at the rank of assistant professor and with satisfactory performance earn the rank of associate professor with tenure. Subsequent to earning tenure with promotion as an associate professor, post-tenure aspirations include obtaining the rank of full professor, the highest rank in the discipline or area (McGowan 2010).

Once Dr. Badger decided to accept a position in higher education, she began to search for publication opportunities having received excellent advice that her dissertation should serve as a platform for publishing her first two to three articles. With little guidance on which publications to include in her search, by chance, Dr. Badger came across the *Teacher Education Journal of South Carolina* (*TEJSC*), a regional South Carolina peer-reviewed journal that includes manuscripts for publication from published authors in addition to manuscripts from graduate students and other new writers. *TEJSC* currently accepts manuscripts twice a year and is jointly published by the South Carolina Association of Teacher Educators (SCATE) and the South Carolina Association of Colleges for Teacher Education (SCACTE). Dr. Badger was fortunate to have her first publication, "The Cultural Symphony in Schools: Effectively Teaching African American and Latino High School Students," completed within the first month of her appointment to her first tenure-track position in higher education.

DR. BADGER'S FIRST BOOK

Even though Dr. Badger has always enjoyed writing, as is the case for many others, writing her first book was still a daunting task. Dr. Badger began with a topic that she was passionate about—how expert principals make difficult decisions—which was deeply connected to her own development as a leader and included a measure of transparency. Dr. Badger decided to conduct a research study of twenty-one principals from five districts in urban and suburban counties in Massachusetts, Maryland, and North Carolina.

Central Office Administrators were asked to recommend their best (expert) principals. In cases where the district expressed reluctance to name best principals, principals were selected who had been mentor principals and/or whose school's standardized test scores reflected above average school achievement for the district. Individual qualitative principal interviews (45–60 minutes) were conducted with principals in five districts in urban and suburban counties. (McLaughlin 2015, 3–4)

Dr. Badger stated that she didn't realize initially just how critical decision-making was to her success. She succumbed to pressure and made hasty decisions without anticipating the likely repercussions. So the book wasn't written to show how much she knew about decision-making but rather what she had learned. Dr. Badger posited that if school leaders are exposed to difficult decisions and their resolutions, they will be better able to solve similar problems. In the book, principals describe the factors they consider in their decision-making as well as a wide range of decisions. The book proposal that Dr. Badger submitted to Corwin Press included a working title, the project overview, marketing ideas, approach/style of presentation, goals of the book, features and benefits, the target audience, strengths of the book, artwork/design, format, competition, the table of contents with chapter highlights, a sample chapter, and references.

After writing a 161-page dissertation, Dr. Badger had already done a lot of writing, but writing a dissertation is a very different type of writing. The importance of favor, timing, and collegial relationships cannot be overstated. After compiling her research, Dr. Badger was in the department office talking with the endowed professor of education, Dr. Gail L. Thompson, and struck up a conversation about her interest in writing a book. Dr. Thompson offered to introduce her to her publisher at Corwin, Dan Alpert, who then subsequently introduced her to Arnis E. Burvikovs, executive editor (now retired).

When Dr. Badger contacted Arnis, he did not respond initially. Dr. Badger mentioned that she would be attending the American Educational Research Association (AERA) Conference in San Francisco and suggested scheduling a meeting at the conference. It is fairly common for editors to attend national conferences, so these conferences can also be an opportunity for authors to shop their book. After Arnis's feedback during their meeting, Dr. Badger submitted a prospectus. She did not hear from Arnis for several weeks, but then she received an email telling her that she had a book contract. It took Dr. Badger about a year to write the book.

MISSED OPPORTUNITY

Several months after completing her first book, Dr. Badger began to think about writing another book. She received an unexpected email from Susan Hills, an acquisitions editor from the Association for Supervision and Curriculum Development (ASCD), who noticed that Dr. Badger was scheduled to present in Long Beach at the National Association of Elementary School Principals (NAESP) conference on decisions from expert principals that led to improved performance among African American and Latinx students. Susan mentioned that unfortunately she had a scheduling conflict and could not attend Dr. Badger's session but that she would like to try to find a time to meet. Susan included the ASCD's book proposal guidelines and asked about Dr. Badger's availability to meet. Susan asked Dr. Badger to meet with her about the feasibility of writing a book for the ASCD. Susan added that ASCD was seeking to grow its list of resources for leaders in education and therefore planned to attend the NAESP conference.

Dr. Badger squandered a great opportunity to publish with ASCD because at the time she had not yet completed her research, so she really was not ready to submit a prospectus. Even though Dr. Badger was invited to submit the prospectus, it was not well developed and ultimately was not accepted for publication. Had Dr. Badger not worried about missing the opportunity and instead indicated that she needed a significant amount of time to complete a well-written prospectus, she might have been able to publish her second book with ASCD. One rejection, however, did not stop Dr. Badger for approaching other publishers.

SECOND BOOK AND OTHER PUBLICATION PROJECTS

Dr. Badger's first mentor and her former dissertation chair, Dr. Fenwick W. English, invited her to participate in several writing projects and encouraged her to join the International Council of Professors of Educational Leadership (ICPEL). Dr. Badger met the late Dr. Sherwood Thompson (no relation to Dr. Gail L. Thompson) at an ICPEL Conference in Charlotte, North Carolina. Given the small size of the conference, it was a great opportunity to connect with other colleagues, particularly colleagues of color. While chatting with Dr. Thompson and other colleagues over lunch, Dr. Badger unabashedly discussed her interest in writing another book. Dr. Sherwood Thompson offered to introduce Dr. Badger to his editor. Dr. Thompson encouraged Dr. Badger to send an email to Kim Chadwick (Emerald Publishing, senior commissioning editor, education), and include his name in the subject line.

Without this amiable gesture and timely advice, Dr. Badger's book prospectus could have languished for months among the hundreds of unsolicited emails that acquisitions editors receive every day. Dr. Badger is incredibly fortunate to have made the acquaintance of Black full professors who supported her writing aspirations as an untenured assistant professor.

One of the keys to publishing both books was conducting relevant research in order to have a plethora of captivating material to write about. As a Black bilingual educator and former principal, Dr. Badger indicated that she found the low levels of proficiency for Black and Latinx students to be disconcerting. Dr. Badger refused to accept the notion that somehow African American and Latinx students cannot compete at the highest levels. She was confident that some of her colleagues in the field had found success in their work with Black and Latinx students, but their stories were simply not being told.

Dr. Badger's second book was created from conversations with eighteen principals in elementary, middle, and high schools in urban and suburban communities in two states that have demonstrated academic success with students of color in their buildings. The principals all lead a nationally or regionally recognized school that has significantly increased the achievement of African American and Latinx students. Non-magnet public schools where 80 percent or more of both the school's African American and Latinx students are proficient on the state's standardized English and math assessments were selected. The book includes cases based on real experiences from K–12 school principals. Dr. Badger investigated eight strategies for leading equitable, high-achieving schools where Black and Latinx students excel (McLaughlin 2020, 1–2).

TIME TO WRITE

Dr. Sherwood Thompson told Dr. Badger that he writes every day even if it is only for fifteen minutes. Dr. Badger admits that she has not quite reached that level of discipline, but she reserves Fridays for writing, and when she is pushing out a publication, she dedicates four to five days a week, sometimes eight to eleven or more hours a day to writing. At that pace, it takes Dr. Badger about twelve months to complete a book. Dr. Badger has worked full-time while writing each of her first two books.

MAKING TIME FOR TEACHING AND SERVICE

The other aspects of making adequate progress toward tenure include service and teaching. In terms of service, Dr. Badger sought opportunities to join university committees. Chairing a subcommittee of the University Graduate Council allowed her to meet and work closely with the graduate school dean and deans from other schools across campus. To a lesser extent, Dr. Badger also provided professional development for a local school district. That type of district collaboration became more of a priority after her fifth year. Every year, however, Dr. Badger participated in conferences and presented her research regionally and nationally.

In terms of teaching, given that she works with aspiring principals, Dr. Badger's classes focus on case studies and other real examples from her work as a former principal and assistant principal. Dr. Badger also invests a considerable amount of time creating interactive lessons, and at the end of each semester, she asks students for feedback about what she did well and what she can improve on; then she makes the adjustments. Teaching is of course a vital part of work in academia, and garnering very strong student evaluations is an absolute must.

FEW BLACK TENURED FACULTY

In 2018 at degree-granting postsecondary institutions, only 2 percent of full professors were Black females, and 2 percent were Black males. For associate professors, 3 percent were Black females and 3 percent were Black males. With regard to assistant professors, while still woefully underrepresented, the numbers were slightly higher: 5 percent were Black females and 3 percent Black males (Hussar et al. 2020).

The aforementioned statistics highlight the reality that the presence of a Black female tenured or tenure-track professor at the rank of full, associate, or assistant is a rarity. Although an anomaly, Dr. Badger overcame the odds and obtained tenure and promotion in 2021. The story of her publishing journey is documented here in hopes of sharing strategies for publishing that junior faculty can utilize to join the ranks of other tenured Black faculty in the academy.

ADVICE FOR NON-TENURED FACULTY

Gentry and Stokes (2015) assert that "scholarship expectations for tenure and promotion to associate professor vary more across discipline and institutions than do those for teaching or service" (quoted in Price and Cotton 2006). The requirements also vary by type of institution (graduate, comprehensive, or undergraduate) and even within types of institutions. The time limit is usually six years to apply for tenure and associate professor. The applicant is expected to compile and submit a portfolio of accomplishments for review in the university evaluation process and is ultimately informed of the results and recommendation by the provost or president (Mabrouk 2007, 4).

In your first year as an assistant or associate professor, it is important to review the tenure and promotion guidelines, determine how points are calculated, and prepare a strong electronic packet for reappointment. While the tenure and promotion guidelines will certainly vary in each institution, it is important to know that tenured colleagues will chair tenure and promotion department, school, and university committees, so their support of your work is critical. It is incredibly important to cultivate relationships with university colleagues by conversing during office hours as well as before and after faculty meetings, and collaborating with other professors through committee work. Connections can also be made by expressing genuine interest in a colleague's children, vacation plans, research interests, or general well-being.

Make sure that you are well liked and well known, and don't be too opinionated, or that could be your downfall. While you may be tempted to pontificate in a faculty meeting or express divergent views, reserve those conversations for trusted colleagues in a one-on-one setting, or share those opinions with a family member or trusted friend outside of campus. Although you may yearn to find a place at work to express your unadulterated views or to just be yourself, do not take any unnecessary risks until you are tenured. It will do you no good if you express those views only to find yourself not reappointed or not tenured seemingly without cause. This notion is supported by Mitchell and Miller (2011), who assert that "for women of color there is an additional layer to their struggles that is predicated on the impact of race and ethnicity, all synergistically affecting how women of color enter, negotiate, and are retained within academia. Themes around the issues that require women of color to subjugate themselves to succeed and find acceptance in academia" (193).

Arm yourself with more than the required number of publications, so you can be confident about reappointment, tenure, and promotion. Join university-wide committees; if time permits, get nominated or elected to faculty senate. If you need to choose between writing a grant or writing a book chapter, the book chapter should always take precedence. As much as you may want to participate in the grant-writing process, reserve grant writing for year five or six or until after you have received tenure. A final word of advice about publishing: don't be afraid to ask for help. Most professors in the academy, though incredibly busy with their own writing projects, are often willing to help.

> If you are going to be a writer there is nothing I can say to stop you; if you're not going to be a writer nothing I can say will help you. What you really need at the beginning is somebody to let you know that the effort is real. —James Baldwin (1989, 251)

REFERENCES

Baldwin, James. 1989. "The Art of Fiction LXXVIII: James Baldwin." Interview by Jordan Elgrably and George Plimpton. In *Conversations with James Baldwin*, edited by Fred L. Standley and Louis H. Pratt, 251. Jackson: University Press of Mississippi.

Gentry, Ruben, and Dorothy Stokes. 2015. "Strategies for Professors Who Service the University to Earn Tenure and Promotion." *Research in Higher Education Journal*, no. 29: 1–13.

Hussar, Bill, Jijun Zhang, Sarah Hein, Ke Wang, Ashley Roberts, Jiashan Cui, Mary Smith, Farrah Bullock Mann, Amy Barmer, and Rita Dilig. 2020. *The Condition of Education* (NCES 2020-144). Washington, DC: U.S. Department of Education, National Center for Education Statistics.

Mabrouk, Patricia Ann. 2007. "Promotion from Associate to Full Professor." *Analytical & Bioanalytical Chemistry* 388, nos. 5/6: 987–91.

McGowan, John. 2010. "An Immodest Proposal." *Quarterly Journal of Speech* 96, no. 4: 413–20.

McLaughlin, Dionne. 2015. *Insights: How Expert Principals Make Difficult Decisions*. Thousand Oaks, CA: Corwin.

McLaughlin, Dionne. 2020. *Personalized Principal Leadership Practices: Eight Strategies for Leading Equitable, High Achieving Schools*. Bingley, UK: Emerald Publishing.

Mitchell, Natasha, and Jaronda Miller. 2011. "The Unwritten Rules of the Academy: A Balancing Act for Women of Color." In *Women of Color in Higher Education: Changing Directions and New Perspectives*, edited by G. Jean-Marie and B. Lloyd-Jones, 193–218. Bingley, UK: Emerald Publishing.

Price, Jamie, and Sheila Cotton. 2006. "Teaching, Research, and Service: Expectations of Assistant Professors." *The American Sociologist* 37, no. 1: 5–21.

Afterword

"You can't have relationships with other people until you give birth to yourself." These words from poet Sonia Sanchez (1999)—retired professor and poet-in-residence at my alma mater, Temple University—were brought to mind and give meaning to the artfully depicted journeys recounted in *The Ivory Tower: Perspectives of Women of Color in Higher Education*. These first-hand experiences of women of color in the academy offer insights into the thoughts and, more importantly, the feelings that emerged and deepened learning and wisdom during their respective journeys. Each chapter reflects on their quests, achievements, and challenges to contribute their talent, knowledge, and expertise to higher education—earning a seat at the table.

Such accounts are needed to help dispel stereotypes and myths about women of color and the possibilities available for them in the academy. In *The Ivory Tower*, we are given a rare glimpse into the complexities of higher education and the imposed kaleidoscope of pathways women of color navigate to achieve recognition and to advance in academia.

I am reminded of women exemplars of my generation, like Sanchez, for the outspoken, confident, and authentic presence they offered to learners during the 1970s—a time when the political climate was charged from scandals, concerns for voting rights, the conclusion of the Vietnam War, an emerging technological revolution, and the early beginnings of video games. In the latter part of the decade, we also faced the serious threat of a possible nuclear disaster as the nearby Three-Mile Island experienced a partial meltdown in 1979.

Likewise, today we see circumstances and societal challenges not too dissimilar to the sociopolitical climate of the 1970s. It is in part IV that the book's authors delve into the issues of our time to explore the rise in concerns for diversity, equity, and inclusion and the experiences of women of color—seeking to find the tools to navigate the rapidly changing landscape for higher education.

Each author offers an illustrative firsthand perspective of the complexities women of color face, especially across the spectrum of higher education. Data from the National Center for Education Statistics (2021) remind us that progress has been made, with statistics showing more women seeking higher education and achieving master's degrees. Yet, in spite of all the gains, full equity and parity remains elusive.

The images these chapters bring to life also show promise for women of color and the future of higher education. There is now greater attention paid to the value of diversity in light of recent events—the pandemic, the rise in violence and social injustice, and the intersectionality of the two crises.

The chapters in parts I and II especially help illuminate the obstacles as well as the opportunities for women to find support and guidance through traditional hiring, promotion, and tenure practices and protocols. However, the authors demonstrate through their own accounts the need for more intentional effort. Basic mentoring and sponsorship opportunities are described as assets toward not only surviving in academia but also thriving and achieving greater success as women of color. Still, such structured programs are rare finds for women of color in the academic setting, especially at the graduate level.

Isolation is a common theme throughout the chapters. This is not surprising when you consider the actual numbers of women of color advancing through the ranks of promotion and tenure. We see few women of color administrators at senior leadership levels, but colleges and universities with female presidents have higher percentages of women in all top administrative categories, according to the College and University Professional Association for Human Resources (Fuesting, Bichsel, and Schmidt 2022). Data from the National Center for Education Statistics show that in 2017, women identifying as Black, Hispanic, Asian, Pacific Islander, or American Indian/Alaskan Native made up 18.3 percent of full-time professors at U.S. universities.

Those numbers increased slightly for women working as associate (24 percent) and assistant (27.5 percent) professors (Snyder, de Brey, and Dillow 2019).

Rather than bemoan the plight of women in higher education throughout history, we should celebrate the resilience of women who took the field by force. Women like Mary McCleod Bethune, one of my "sheroes," broke down barriers during some of the most challenging times in our country for African Americans. And her "Head, Heart and Hands" framework disarmed even the staunchest of her opponents to create intentional acts and structures that support "sisterly collaboration." Other powerful women joining Bethune in the fight include:

- Fannie Coppin: a teacher, principal, and lecturer who became a beacon by which future generations would set their courses;
- Lucy Laney: a teacher, lecturer, and school founder; and
- Marian Wright Edelman, a lifelong advocate for the rights of disadvantaged Americans.

These are just some of the figures brought to mind while each chapter delivers its own perspective on the world of women of color in the academy.

The chapters also highlight the often-higher standards that women of color are called to uphold in our society—creating the superwoman schema (SWS; Woods-Griscome 2010), where women convince themselves they must be all things to all people. It is that nurturing and socializing manner that Lynch, Brittingham Barnett, and Green speak to in their chapter: "Watching and Waiting to Exhale: Affirming Black Women in Academia." It is this account that calls to mind my own experiences as a doctoral student. When asked how I managed to work full time, go to school full time, and raise my children, my small attempt at humor was the reply, "Sleep is often overrated." The SWS approach to climbing the academic career ladder speaks to what one author refers to as the "service to others" impact, which she appropriately identifies as a potential risk to the wellness of Black women. It is nonetheless a well-known and experienced phenomenon of women of color, who hold themselves to the highest of standards. The downside to such high aspirations can, as described in the chapter, overlook the much-needed self-care required to reach the long horizons of the academic career ladder. It also takes an emotional toll when women of color experience failure due to unrealistic expectations they set for themselves.

Diversity, equity, and inclusion (DEI) has taken on new meaning and is a primary focus across all industries, as well as business and government entities. These accounts of the experiences of women of color in higher education offer insights to leaders and administrators seeking to advance DEI on their campuses. Why the emphasis on diversity, equity and inclusion for higher education? While there is a growing concern for the lack of diversity and inclusion in all workplaces, higher education presents unique challenges to women of color. Race and gender play a critical role in shaping the thinking and planning for women's careers in the academy today and what we have learned from the past. Not having role models in the classrooms has been shown to have a detrimental impact to the perceived efficacy and to overall student development. Role models encourage students and aspiring young professionals to see the possibilities. Undergraduates and graduate students alike benefit when they are able to look up to someone who reflects their own identities.

Inclusion, on the other hand, surpasses representation and promotes a sense of connectedness, where all feel valued. It offers a deeper connection for all in the campus community to contribute equally; and studies by McKinsey and Company have actually shown a greater return on investment (ROI) in diverse organizations and point to more than altruistic reasons for organizations to subscribe to DEI as a goal (Dixon-Fyle et al. 2020).

By bringing to light the lack of diversity and inclusion of women of color, the authors offer hope for a solution to meet the changing landscape and workforce needs toward a more inclusive pathway for women of color in the academy.

We honor those who came before by opening the door to the future. I am honored to serve as president of the oldest HBCU in the state of Maryland. As the tenth president of Bowie State University and the first woman to hold the position, I recognize I am a member of a small sisterhood of women of color presidents who have benefitted from those who came before me and paved the way. As of 2016, 30 percent of college presidents were women, although women make up more than 50 percent of the college student population; and of that number, 5 percent are Black, while 17 percent are classified as racial minorities (American Council on Education 2017). According to the Thurgood Marshall College Fund and the United Negro College Fund (cited in Eversley, 2019), women made up just 25 percent of HBCU presidents in 2019. It is my belief that each of us in our small band of women of color leaders owes it to the next generation to create that sense of belonging for those coming up the ladder of academia.

The road ahead for this generation is still fraught with inequities in promotion and tenure rates, and the salaries of women are not equitable with that of men—although female senior faculty and top administrators earn more at institutions with female presidents and provosts than institutions where men are in charge, according to the College and University Professional Association for Human Resources (Fuesting et al. 2022).

The chapters presented here in *The Ivory Tower* are a testament to the resilience and drive of bright and talented women of the academy. Their chapters should remind us that the work continues. And their stories should encourage us to press on carrying the legacies of a special sisterhood striving to find their well-earned and rightful place in the academy.

Aminta H. Breaux,
Tenth President of Bowie State University

REFERENCES

American Council on Education. 2017. *American College President Study 2017*. www.aceacps.org/summary-profile-dashboard.

Dixon-Fyle, Sundiatu, Kevin Dolan, Vivian Hunt, and Sara Prince. 2020, May 19. "Diversity Wins: How Inclusion Matters." McKinsey and Company. www.mckinsey.com/featured-insights/diversity-and-inclusion/diversity-wins-how-inclusion-matters.

Eversley, Melanie. 2019, March 1. "Changing HERstory." *Currents Magazine*. www.case.org/resources/issues/march-april-2019/changing-herstory.

Fuesting, Melissa, Jacqueline Bichsel, and Anthony Schmidt. 2022, January. "Women in the Leadership Pipeline in Higher Education Have Better Representation and Pay in Institutions with Female Presidents and Provosts." College and University Professional Association for Human Resources. www.cupahr.org/surveys/research-briefs/women-executives-in-higher-ed.

National Center for Education Statistics. 2021. *Condition of Education*. U.S. Department of Education, Institute of Education Sciences. https://nces.ed.gov/programs/coe/indicator/ctb.

Sanchez, Sonia. 1999. "Shake Loose My Skin." In *Shake Loose My Skin: New and Selected Poems*. Boston, MA: Beacon Press.

Snyder, T. D., C. de Brey, and S. A. Dillow. 2019. "Table 315.20. Full-Time Faculty in Degree-Granting Postsecondary Institutions, by Race/Ethnicity, Sex, and Academic Rank: Fall 2015, Fall 2016, and Fall 2017." In *Digest of Education Statistics 2018* (NCES 2020-009), 291. Washington, DC: National Center for Education Statistics, Institute of Education Sciences, U.S. Department of Education. https://nces.ed.gov/pubs2020/2020009.pdf.

Woods-Griscome, C. 2010. *Superwoman Schema: African American Women's Views on Stress, Strength, and Health*. Quality Health Research.

Index

Abolition for the People
(Kaepernick), 62–63
abolition teaching, 132, 136
academic advising, 96
academic self-concept: developing,
114–15; of Lelia, 118
"Accents" (Frohman), 120
ACT. *See* Afrocentric values
Adela: background, 119; mentor-
mentee relationships and, 119–20;
networks and, 120
Adichie, Chimamanda Ngozi, 63
administration: Black female
mathematician and, 180; noise of,
180–81; Rashida and, 26; SWS
and, 9; theme, ix
advancement: hazing, 10; HBCUs
and, 9–10; in LIS, 163; overview
of topics, 2; theme, ix, x–xi. *See
also* promotion
affinity groups: IM and, 77; margins
and, 17–18; Retaining Each Other
Framework and, 82
affirmative action, 126–27
African American scholars, 133–34
Afrocentric values (ACT): Black
History Week, 128–30; CRC

and, 127; CRT and, 126–27;
discussion, 136–37; Eurocentric
scholarship and, 127–28;
introduction, 125–26; IT and,
126; joy and, 128; mentoring
undergraduate research students,
134–36; mentorship and, 125–37;
secret society mentorship,
130–32; theoretical perspectives,
126–28
age discrimination: hurt from, 81;
theme, x
Agyemang, Mavis: extramural
grant and, 52; graduate school
experience, 45–46; at HBCUs,
44; as junior faculty, 51–52;
pearls of wisdom, 52–53;
pharmacy education and,
43–44, 45–46, 48–49, 51–52;
postdoctoral experience, 48–49;
undergraduate experience, 43–44
ALA. *See* American Library
Association
American Civil War, 125
American Library Association
(ALA), 161–62
Asante, Molefe, 127–28

ASCD. *See* Association for Supervision and Curriculum Development

assignments, 154

Association for Supervision and Curriculum Development (ASCD), 188

authenticity, 177

Badger, Denise: first book of, 186–88; habits of writing, 190; introduction, 185–86; make time for teaching and service, 190; publishing journey of, 185–92; second book and other projects, 188–90; tenure statistics related to, 191

Bailey, Moya, 165

Baldwin, James, 192

Battle, Dolores, 103

Benbow, Candice, 151

Bethune, Mary McCleod, 197

Beyoncé, 151

BFT. *See* Black feminist thought

Binghamton University, SUNY, 176

BIPOC. *See* Black Indigenous People of Color

Black Athena (Bernal), 129

Black feminist thought (BFT): explained, 76; features of, 8; IM and, 76–77; womanism and, 77

Black Feminist Thought (Collins), 72

Black History Week, 128–30

Black Indigenous People of Color (BIPOC): dearth of faculty, 93; safe haven for, 39–40; stress and, 39. *See also specific topics*

Black men, microaggressions of, 16

Black women: affinity groups, 17–18; as alone, 7–8; HBCUs and, 9–10; identity and, 7; margins embraced by, 17–18; as protectors, 9, 21, 63; seat of honor, 20–21; social constructs and, 7–10; storytelling and, 8, 18–19; unbothered, 19; uphill battle of, 7–8. *See also specific topics*

Black Women's Club Movement, 81

bonding function, 41

boundaries: healthy, 182; introduction, 151–52; JOY and, 155–57; as necessary, 157–58; rationale for establishing, 152–54; tasks, assignments, opportunities and, 154–55

Bourdieu, P., 40–41

Bowie State University, 134

Br'er Rabbit storytelling, 133

bridging function, 41

Brown, John, 137

Burke, Tarana, 62

Burvikovs, Arnis E., 187–88

CAE. *See* critical autoethnography

Cao, Jing, 105

CAU. *See* Clark Atlanta University

Center for Community Organizations, 164

Chadwick, Kim, 189

Chicago Defender newspaper, 131–32

Civil War. *See* American Civil War

Clark Atlanta University (CAU), 162, 164–65

Clarke: as exploited, 10; extracurricular activities and, 11; on performance evaluation, 11–12; resentment and, 11; storytelling and, 18–19; SWS and, 10–12 clinical faculty: BIPOC and, 98–99; clinical education and, 94–95; duties, 94; introduction, 93–94; research/teaching and, 95

Collins, Patricia Hill, 8, 17, 72, 131

The Color Purple, 20

community: Center for Community Organizations, 164; find/build, 182; mother, 131–32; Rashida and, 35; support via, 35

competition: Rashida and, 26, 33; speech, 131; support system and, 33

Contraband soldiers, 125

Cookie: academic abandonment, 12–15; gaslit, 14; guard let down, 13; sponsor disappointing, 13–14; storytelling and, 18–19; as troublemaker, 12–15

Cooper, Brittney: on joy, 152; on self-love, 151

Coppin, Fannie, 197

Corley, Jacquelyn, 25, 26

Covey, Stephen, 64

COVID-19, ix; Black female mathematician and, 180–81; inequities from, 34; Rashida and, 33, 34–35; Zoom and, 34–35

CRC. *See* culturally relevant care

crecimiento (growth), 141, *145*, 146

critical autoethnography (CAE), 82

critical inquiry, 98

critical librarianship, 167

critical praxis, 98

critical race theory (CRT), 126–27

crystal stair, 159–60

culturally relevant care (CRC), 127

Danielle: conclusion, 89–90; HWI and, 82, 86; imposter syndrome and, 89; mentorship and, 83; outsider status and, 88–89; question self and establish trust, 85–86; racialized spaces navigated, 86–88; sister circle work party and, 84–89; story of, 82–83

Davis, Shametrice, 30–31, 32–33

deficit models: CRC, 127; CRT, 126–27; IT, 126

dehumanization, 62

DEI. *See* diversity, equity, and inclusion

diversity: HBCUs and, *27*, 27–28; LIS narrative of, 160

diversity, equity, and inclusion (DEI), 198

Diversity and Inclusion in Libraries (Jones and Murphy), 161

doctoral programs, 25–26

documentation, 182

domestic violence, 60

Edelman, Marian Wright, 197

Egypt, 129

Emory University, 166

empowerment: BFT and, 8; of others, 180–81, 183; women of color and, 1–3, 81

endarkened epistemologies, 72

engineer analogy, 109–10

English, Fenwick W., 188–89

entendimiento (understanding), 142, *145*

Eurocentric scholarship, 127–28

extracurricular activities: Agyemang and, 52; Clarke and, 11

faculty: dearth of BIPOC, 93; gender statistics, 93; race/ethnicity example, *27*; retention issues, 103. *See also* clinical faculty; junior faculty; tenure-track faculty; White faculty

failure, fear of, 174, 175–76

Farmer, Jennifer, 60

feminism, x; BFT, 8, 72, 76–77; mascots and, 62

Fisher v. University of Texas, 27

Florence, Virginia Proctor Powell, 161

Fortune 500 companies, 60

Fries-Britt, Sharon, 86

Frohman, Denice, 120

Fugitive Pedagogy (Givens), 125

game analogy, 96

Garner, Lula, 130, 131–32

gaslighting, 14

gender: cultural studies and, 99; faculty statistics on, 93; hard work due to, 86; LIS and, 159; mentorship and, xi, 172; role models and, 198; theme, ix

generational trauma, 59–60

Gil, Elizabeth, 107–8

Givens, Jarvis, 125, 126

goals: focus on, 36; short- and long-term, 172

Gomez, M., 128

Gorman, Amanda, 177

graduate students: Agyemang, 45–46; Hernandez, 44–45; Martinez, 45; theme, xi

growth. *See crecimiento*

Hale, Angelica, 162

Hamer, Fannie Lou, 129, 131

Hannah-Jones, Nikole, ix, 8

Harris, Kamala, 28

hatred/prejudice directed toward Black women. *See misogynoir*

hazing, 10

HBCUs. *See* Historically Black Colleges and Universities

Head, Heart and Hands framework, 197

Hernandez, Camila: graduate school experience, 44–45; imposter syndrome and, 44–45; as junior faculty, 49–50; pearls of wisdom, 52–53; pharmacy education and, 42–43, 44–45, 46–47, 49–50; postdoctoral experience, 46–47; undergraduate experience, 42–43

Herrick, Ms., 133–34

highway metaphor, 75–76

Hills, Susan, 188

Historically Black Colleges and Universities (HBCUs): advancement and, 9–10; Agyemang at, 44, 45; Cookie and, 12–15; critical inquiry facilitation, 98; critical praxis and, 98; disheartening experiences at, 9–10; diversity at, *27*, 27–28; faculty race/ethnicity example, *27*; HWIs versus, 97–99; library education programs at, 162; microaggressions at, 16; presidents, 198–99; racialized space navigated in, 87; social justice service and, 98

Historically White Institutions (HWIs): critical inquiry facilitation, 98; critical praxis and, 98; Danielle in, 82, 86; HBCUs versus, 97–99; navigated, 86–88; Renee and, 84, 87; social justice service and, 98

honor, seat of, 20–21
hooks, bell, 81, 153
hope, 136
Hughes, Langston, 159–60
Hurston, Zora Neale, 57, 71
HWIs. *See* Historically White
  Institutions

identity: Black women, 7; collective,
  8. *See also* Latina identity
"If We Must Die" (McKay), 21
IM. *See* intersectionality
  methodology
imposter syndrome: Black female
  mathematician and, 177–81;
  Danielle and, 89; defined, 44;
  Hernandez and, 44–45
inequality, social capital and, 40–41
inspiración (inspiration),
  143–44, *145*
instrumental mentoring: focus of,
  113–14; Lelia and, 118
integration, 126–27
interaction theories (IT), 126
intersectionality: analysis and,
  97–98; BFT and, 8; critical
  inquiry and, 98; critical praxis
  and, 98; defined, 97; "isms"
  explored by, 42; perspective,
  41–42; pharmacy education
  and, 41–42; theme, ix; unequal
  standards and, 25
intersectionality methodology (IM):
  BFT and, 76–77; womanism
  and, 77
invisible hand, 127
Isler, Evangeline Jones Artis, 151
isolation, 7–8, 196
IT. *See* interaction theories

Jackson, Andrew P., 160
Jefferson, Julius, Jr., 160
Jim Crow era, 74–75
joy: boundaries as necessary for,
  158; Love and, 128, 136, 152;
  scholars on, 152; spirituals
  and, 128
JOY mnemonic: J for just, 155–56;
  O for objectives, 156; wholeness
  pursued with, 155–57; Y is it my
  responsibility, 156–57
junior faculty: Agyemang as, 51–52;
  Hernandez as, 49–50; Martinez
  as, 50–51
justice, 155–56

Kaepernick, Colin, 62–63
Kappe, Luise, 176
Keisha: as protector, 15–17;
  sisterhood and, 15–16;
  storytelling and, 18–19; strength
  in numbers, 15–17
Kelly, Bridget Turner, 86
King Richard, 62
Kovalevsky, Sonia, 177
Kutzko, Phil, 175

Lacks, Henrietta, 59
Ladson-Billings, Gloria, 76
Laney, Lucy, 197
Latina identity: *crecimiento* and,
  141, *145*, 146; *entendimiento*
  and, 142, *145*; *inspiración* and,
  143–44, *145*; introduction, 141;
  movimiento and, 142–43, *145*;
  reflección and, 144–46, *145*
leadership, 165–67, 179
Lee, Tiffany S., 97
Lelia: academic self-concept of,
  118; lab environment of, 118;

in mentor-mentee relationships, 117–19; perseverance of, 117–18, 119

Lemonade, 151

Leslie, Joshua, 133, 134–35

library and information science (LIS): advancement in, 163; author experience in, 164–65; critical librarianship, 167; crystal stair and, 159–60; demographics and history, 161–62; diversity narrative of, 160; diversity-related initiatives, 162–63; gender and, 159; introduction, 159–61; leadership path and, 165–67; texts on, 160–61; transgressions called out in, 167; White supremacy and, 159

Lima, Sharon, 175

LIS. *See* library and information science

Lorde, Audre, 65, 157–58

Louisville Free Public Library Negro Branch, 161

Love, Bettina: abolitionist teacher and, 132; enslaved ancestors and, 128; joy and, 128, 136, 152; *We Want to Do More Than Survive* by, 125–26

Mammies, 152

Manderscheid, David, 176

Martinez, Skye: graduate school experience, 45; as junior faculty, 50–51; pearls of wisdom, 52–53; pharmacy education, 43, 45, 47–48, 50–51; postdoctoral experience, 47–48; undergraduate experience, 43

mascots, 62

mathematician, Black female: academia navigation strategies, 172–73; administration and, 180; authenticity of, 177; awards, 178–79; background of, 173–74; books recommended by, 179; COVID-19 and, 180–81; fear of failure, 175–76; impostor syndrome and, 177–81; introduction, 171–72; leadership of, 179; lessons learned, 181, 183; McBay and, 174–75; noise impacting, 180–81; as only one, 181–83; as perfectionist, 173–77; portfolio kept by, 175; success focus of, 178–80; at UI, 175–76; at UWEC, 177, 178–80; value added by, 183

Matias, J. Nathan, x

McBay, Shirley, 174–75

McKay, Claude, 21

mentor-mentee relationships: academic self-concept and, 114–15; Adela, 119–20; belonging and, 115–16; continuum, 113–14; critical nature of, 114–17; development of effective, 120–21; instrumental and psychosocial, 113–14, 118; introduction, 113; Lelia, 117–19; network building, 116–17; synergistic nature of, 114

mentorship: academia navigated via, 172; ACT values and, 125–37; of African American scholars, 133–34; via ancestor energy force, 132–33; communication issues, 105–6; CRC and, 127; cross-race/gender, xi; cultural mismatch in, 105; Danielle and,

83; defined, 105; expectation issues, 106; gender and, xi, 172; Hatcher on, 173; *inspiración* and, 144; introduction, 104; near-to-peer, 106–7, 109; overview of topics, 2; peer-to-peer, 106, 107, 109; problems with traditional, 105–6; psychosocial, 113–14, 118; race and, xi; *reflección* and, 144–46, *145*; rules surrounding, 105–8; in secret society, 130–32; silence and, 16; spirituals and, 132–33; to sponsorship, 108–9; STEM and, 113, 115, 117–19; SURI and, 134; theme, ix, xi; of undergraduate research students, 134–36
#MeToo movement, 62
Miller, Jaronda, 192
misogynoir (hatred/prejudice directed toward Black women), 165
Mississippi Vocational College (MVC), 131
Mitchell, Natasha, 192
Moorhead, Mississippi: Black History Week and, 128–30; secret society and, 130–32
Morton, Benterah C., 107–8
"Mother to Son" (Hughes), 159–60
Mount Ararat Church, 130
movimiento (movement), 142–43, *145*
mule metaphor, 71, 73–74
MVC. *See* Mississippi Vocational College

NAESP. *See* National Association of Elementary School Principals
Nanny, 71, 74, 75

Narrative and the Caring Professions course, 94–95
National Association of Elementary School Principals (NAESP), 188
National Center for Education Statistics, 25, 93
National Science Foundation (NSF), 174
near-to-peer mentoring: early career faculty and, 106–7; mid-career and senior faculty, 107; SWOT analysis and, 109
networks: academia navigated via, 172; Adela using, 120; *inspiración* and, 143–44; mentor-mentee relationships and, 116–17
Niger/Congolese Africans, 128, 133, 134–35, 137
noise, 180–81
NSF. *See* National Science Foundation

Obama, Michelle, 183
objectives, 156
opportunities, 155
Otto, Carolyn, 177

pay it forward, 53
peer-to-peer mentoring, 106; group support via, 107; SWOT analysis and, 109
perfectionist: authenticity and, 177; Black female mathematician as, 173–77; fear of failure, 174, 175–76
performance evaluation, 11–12
perseverance: via challenge, 25–36; Lelia, 117–18, 119; resilience and, 39

pharmacy education: Agyemang
    and, 43–44, 45–46, 48–49,
    51–52; conceptual framework
    related to, 40–42; Hernandez
    and, 42–43, 44–45, 46–47,
    49–50; institutional fit and, 52;
    intersectional perspective, 41–42;
    Martinez and, 43, 45, 47–48,
    50–51; pay it forward, 53; pearls
    of wisdom, 52–53; social capital
    perspectives, 40–41
Pho, Annie, 160–61
Pleasant Green Church, 130–31
political no, 96
postdoctoral experiences:
    Agyemang, 48–49; Hernandez,
    46–47; Martinez, 47–48
Predominantly White Institutions
    (PWIs), 9; imposter syndrome
    and, 44; Martinez at, 43
presidents, college, 198–99
pride, 53
promotion: Cookie and, 12–15;
    hazing, 10; overview of topics, 2;
    theme, ix
protectors: Black women as, 9, 21,
    63; Keisha, 15–17
psychosocial mentoring: focus of,
    113–14; Lelia and, 118
publishing: advice related to,
    191–92; Badger's first book,
    186–88; Badger's second book
    and other projects, 188–90; habits
    of writing, 190; journey, 185–92
Pushing the Margins (Chou and
    Pho), 160–61
Putnam, R. D., 41
PWIs. *See* Predominantly White
    Institutions

Quality Education for Minorities
    (QEM), 174

racial battle fatigue, 47, 48, 157
racially charged issues, 29
racism: as pandemic, ix; racialized
    spaces navigated, 86–88;
    responsibility and, 157
Rashida: administration and, 26;
    allies unexpected by, 31–33;
    Black cohort and, 32; community
    and, 35; competition and, 26,
    33; COVID 19 and, 33, 34–35;
    diversity and, *27*, 27–29, *28*;
    doctoral cohort of, *28*, 28–29;
    goal focus of, 36; lessons learned,
    35–36; microaggressions and,
    29–30; program practices and,
    27–31; racially charged issues
    and, 29; relaxation and, 36;
    socioeconomic background, 30;
    successes of, 26; TED talk and,
    30; true to self, 35; underdog and,
    25; White students and, 33
reflección (reflection), 144–46, *145*
relax, 36
Renee: HWI and, 84; outsider status
    and, 88–89; question self and
    establish trust, 85–86; racialized
    spaces navigated, 86–88; sister
    circle work party and, 84–89;
    story of, 83–84
resilience: celebrating, 197; LIS and,
    167; perseverance and, 39; strong
    Black woman schema and, 50;
    theme, ix
resistance: harm from, 59–60; via
    storytelling, 18–19
responsibility, 156–57

Retaining Each Other Framework, 81–82
retention: culture of university impacting, 1–2; faculty, 103
"Retention of Minority Faculty in Higher Education" (Battle), 103
Rihanna, 15
role models, 198
Rolling Stone magazine, 63
Rucks-Ahidiana, Z., ix–x
rules, academia navigated via, 173

Sanchez, Sonia, 195
science, technology, engineering, and math (STEM): academic self-concept in, 115; Adela in, 119–20; belonging and, 115–16; conceptual framework, 40–42; intersectional perspective, 41–42; Lelia mentored in, 117–19; mentorship access in, 113, 115; network building in, 116–17; social capital perspectives, 40–41; success and, 116; White majority and, 42
secret society mentorship, 130–32
self-love: Cooper on, 151; hooks on, 153; wholeness and, 152
self-preservation, 19
Semester-based Undergraduate Research Institute (SURI), 134
sexism, as pandemic, ix
sexualization, 60–61
Shaw, Stephanie, 72; highway metaphor and, 75; *What a Woman Ought to Be and Do* by, 74–75
Sims, Marian, 59
sister circle: CAE and, 82; conclusion, 89–90; generational difference and, 88; historical creation of, 81; outsider status and, 88–89; question self and establish trust, 85–86; racialized spaces navigated, 86–88; support system, 81; work party, 84–89
sisterhood: close ranks, 20; Keisha and, 15–16; silence and, 16–17; theme, ix; womanism and, 72–73
Slave Culture (Stuckey), 134
social capital: Bourdieu and, 40–41; Putnam and, 41
social justice service, 98
socioeconomic background: ignorance surrounding, 30–31; Rashida, 30
sociopolitical climate, 195–96
Sonia Kovalevsky high school and middle school math day for girls, 177
"Sorry" (song), 151
speech competition, 131
spirituals: joy and, 128; mentorship and, 132–33
sponsorship: Cookie let down by, 13–14; defined, 108; introduction, 104; mentorship to, 108–9
State University of New York (SUNY), 176
STEM. *See* science, technology, engineering, and math
stereotypes, 152–55
storytelling: apprehension surrounding, 8–9; Black women and, 8, 18–19; Br'er Rabbit, 133; resistance via, 18–19
strengths, weaknesses, opportunities, and threats (SWOT analysis), 109–10
stress, 39
strike, 171–72

strong Black woman schema, 50
Stuckey, Sterling, 133–35
SUNY. *See* State University of New York
superwoman schema (SWS): administration and, 9; apologies and, 154; Clarke and, 10–12; conclusions, 197–98; dangers of, 153–54; seat of honor and, 20–21; stereotype rejection, 64
support system: academia navigated via, 172; community and, 35; competition and, 33; pharmacy education and, 52–53; sister circles, 81; theme, ix; unexpected allies, 31–33. *See also* mentor-mentee relationships; mentorship
SURI. *See* Semester-based Undergraduate Research Institute
SWOT analysis. *See* strengths, weaknesses, opportunities, and threats
SWS. *See* superwoman schema

tasks, 154
Taylor, Breonna, 56
Taylor, Julia Mae, 132
Teacher Education Journal of South Carolina (TEJSC), 186
Teaching to Transgress (hooks), 81
TED talk, 30
TEJSC. *See Teacher Education Journal of South Carolina*
tenure: advise related to, 191–92; hazing, 10; journey to, 185–92; LIS and, 166–67; overview of topics, 2; standards, 186; statistics related to, 191; theme, ix, x
tenure-track faculty: academic advising and, 96; BIPOC and, 98–99; duties, 95; game analogy, 96; introduction, 93–94; research and, 95–96
test pilot analogy, 109
Their Eyes Were Watching God (Hurston), 57, 71
Thompson, Gail L., 187
Thompson, Sherwood, 189, 190
thriving: academia navigated via, 173; overview of topics, 2
triple threat, 171–72
troublemaker, 10, 12–15
Turner, Nat, 137
The 21st-Century Black Librarian in America (Jackson, Jefferson and Nosakhere), 160

UI. *See* University of Iowa
underdog, 25
undergraduate experience: Agyemang, 43–44; Hernandez, 42–43; Martinez, 43; mentorship of research students, 134–36
understanding. *See entendimiento*
Unfinished Business (Wheeler), 160
"Universities Say They Want More Diverse Faculties" (Matias), x
University of Iowa (UI), 175–76
University of New Mexico, 97
University of Wisconsin–Eau Claire (UWEC), 177, 178–80
Untold Stories (Tucker), 160
UWEC. *See* University of Wisconsin-Eau Claire

Vasquez Heilig, Julian, 1
Vesey, Denmark, 137
vigilance, 17
voluntold: Black women history and, 59–61; concept, 57–58; culture

resisted, 61–63; generational trauma, 59; introduction, 55–57; military origins, 58; workspaces fight against, 63–65

Walker, Alice, 72–73
We Want to Do More Than Survive (Love), 125–26
What a Woman Ought to Be and Do (Shaw), 74–75
Wheeler, Maurice B., 160, 163
White faculty: African American scholars mentored by, 133–34; unexpected allies, 31–33
White men: in Fortune 500 companies, 60; intersectionality and, 41–42; Martinez and, 47–48
White students: Rashida and, 33; socioeconomic background and, 30–31
White supremacy: invisible hand and, 127; LIS and, 159

"White Supremacy Culture in Organizations" (Center for Community Organizations), 164
White women, #MeToo movement and, 62
wholeness: boundaries as necessary for, 158; JOY pursuing, 155–57; self-love and, 152
Williams, Edward Christopher, 161
Williams, Venus and Serena, 62
womanism: BFT and IM related to, 77; defined, 72–73
women: challenges of, ix–xii; empowering, 1–3, 81; overview of topics, 2; as underrepresented, 1. *See also specific topics*
Woodson, Carter G., 125, 127, 128, 134

Yang, Yu-Chung, 105

Zoom: COVID 19 and, 34–35; interviews using, 35

About the Editors and Contributors

EDITORS

Kimetta R. Hairston, PhD, is the associate vice president for regional centers and online programs at Bowie State University. She received her PhD in curriculum and instruction with an interdisciplinary certificate in diversity and disability studies from the University of Hawaii at Manoa. Her primary research focuses on curriculum and instruction, qualitative research design, diversity, and culturally responsive pedagogy. Dr. Hairston was nominated and served as a 2018–2019 American Council on Education (ACE) fellow. Her commitment to and experience in social justice includes publications on diversity and cultural awareness, Black women in leadership, and the integration of diversity and interdisciplinary studies in K–20 curricula. She is an author and recently published and served as the lead editor for *The Black Experience and Navigating Higher Education in a Virtual World*. One of her many professional accomplishments includes establishing the sole proprietorship of Critical Diverse Interventions (CDI) Consulting, LLC. Over her more than twenty-five years in education, she has published numerous peer-reviewed journal articles, book chapters, and encyclopedia references. Dr. Hairston has also presented at over 150 local, state, national, and international conferences and workshops. She is a proud member of Alpha Kappa Alpha Sorority Inc.

Dr. **Tawannah G. Allen** is an associate professor of educational leadership in the Stout School of Education at High Point University. She has been recognized as the 2021 Higher Education Professional to

Watch by the North Carolina Association of Middle Level Education (NCMLE). Dr. Allen is also a NC Education Policy fellow and is an inaugural cohort member of the Hunt Institute's Elevate NC: Higher Education. As a researcher, Dr. Allen is a member of Bridges2Success (B2S), a research and development lab composed of scholars who are engaged in basic and applied research, focusing on the educational plight of K–20 students of color. As a B2S scholar, Dr. Allen designs and facilitates professional-development training, for school districts and private sector organizations, on the opportunities for and access to postsecondary education for underrepresented students, girls in STEM, stereotyping and implicit biases, and the impact of trauma on academics. Dr. Allen earned a bachelor's degree in psychology, elementary education teacher licensure, and a master of education degree in communication disorders all from North Carolina Central University, while also earning a master of school administration from Fayetteville State University. She earned a graduate certificate in program evaluation from the University of Connecticut (UCONN), and her doctorate in education was earned from the University of North Carolina at Chapel Hill (UNC).

CONTRIBUTORS

Dr. **Comfort Boateng** is an assistant professor in the basic pharmaceutical sciences department at High Point University, in High Point, North Carolina.

Dr. **Kim Brittingham Barnett** is an associate professor in the department of behavioral science and human services at Bowie State University, in Bowie, Maryland.

Angela D. Broadnax, PhD, is currently a visiting professor in the chemistry department at High Point University, in High Point, North Carolina.

Shamella Cromartie, MLS, is associate dean for Hunter Library at Western Carolina University, in Cullowhee, North Carolina.

Dr. **Makeba T. Green** is an associate professor and chair of the department of social work at Bowie State University, in Bowie, Maryland.

Brandi Hinnant-Crawford, PhD, is an associate professor of educational research and the diversity, equity, and inclusion coordinator for teacher education at Western Carolina University, in Cullowhee, North Carolina.

Yolanda F. Holt, PhD, CCC-SLP, is an associate professor of communication sciences and disorders at East Carolina University, in Greenville, North Carolina.

Dr. **Erica-Brittany Horhn** is an English instructor at High Point University, in High Point, North Carolina.

Dr. **Nina Jacks** is an administrator in Prince George's County Public Schools in Upper Marlboro, Maryland.

Dr. **Miyoshi Juergensen** is an assistant professor of teacher leadership at Kennesaw State University, in Kennesaw, Georgia.

Joy L. Kennedy, PhD, CCC-SLP, is an assistant professor in the speech program, speech-language pathology concentration at North Carolina Agricultural and Technical State University in Greensboro, North Carolina.

Dr. **Sharon Lassiter** is an adjunct instructor of English and educator-preparation courses at North Carolina Agricultural and Technical State University in Greensboro, North Carolina.

Dr. **Annie Ruth Leslie** was a former chair in the department of behavioral sciences and human services at Bowie State University in Bowie, Maryland.

Dr. **Dandrielle Lewis** is chair of the mathematical sciences department at High Point University in High Point, North Carolina.

Dr. **Ayanna M. Lynch** is an assistant professor and supportive academic advisor in the department of psychology at Bowie State University in Bowie, Maryland.

Dr. **Dionne V. McLaughlin** is the executive director of the Critical Reflections on Race and Equity Initiative (CRREI) and an associate professor at North Carolina Central University in Durham, North Carolina.

Dr. **Diamond Melendez** is an assistant professor in the clinical sciences department and the director of standardized client experiences at High Point University in High Point, North Carolina.

Dr. **Bianca Nixon** is an assistant professor and the co-curricular director in the clinical sciences department at High Point University in High Point, North Carolina.

Marie Parfait-Davis, EdD, is an equity specialist serving in the Office of Equity with Baltimore City Public Schools in Baltimore, Maryland.

Mariela A. Rodríguez, PhD, is professor and interim department chair of the department of educational leadership and policy studies at the University of Texas at San Antonio.

Verónica A. Segarra, PhD, is an associate professor and the Maryland E-Nnovation Endowed Chair in Biological Sciences and Chemistry at Goucher College in Baltimore, Maryland.

Dr. **Tamela C. Thomas** is an assistant professor of teacher leadership at Kennesaw State University in Kennesaw, Georgia.

Dr. **Shaundra Walker** is an associate professor of library science and the library director at Georgia College in Milledgeville, Georgia.

CPSIA information can be obtained
at www.ICGtesting.com
Printed in the USA
LVHW111917260922
729329LV00004B/230

9 781475 868241